# DON'T MUZZLE THE OX

# FULL-TIME MINISTRY IN LOCAL CHURCHES

# DON'T MUZZLE THE OX

## FULL-TIME MINISTRY IN LOCAL CHURCHES

*Introduced by*

Alan Batchelor

Published for
PARTNERSHIP

by

paternoster
periodicals

**British Library Cataloguing in Publication Data**
A catalogue record for this book is available from the British Library

ISBN 0-900128-19-4

Typeset by WestKey, Falmouth, Cornwall.
Published for Partnership by Paternoster Periodicals,
P.O. Box 300, Carlisle, Cumbria. CA3 0QS and
Printed in the UK by BPC Wheatons Ltd., Exeter, Devon

# CONTENTS

# About Partnership

A fellowship of individuals and churches (mainly with 'Brethren' roots), Partnership's main aim is to encourage the application of biblical principles to the changing conditions of modern life, particularly in the area of church life and witness.

Partnership publishes a magazine, *Partnership Perspectives*, three times a year, a broadsheet, *Partnership Update*, twice a year, and an *International Newsletter*, once a year. It also publishes several books, booklets and study guides each year.

Enquiries regarding individual and church subscriptions should be directed to the executive secretary, **Dr Neil Summerton**, 52 Hornsey Lane, London N5 6LU (Tel: 0171–272–0643).

Further copies of this book, and of other Partnership publications, may be obtained from: Paternoster Periodicals, PO Box 300, Carlisle, Cumbria CA3 0QS (Tel: 01228–512512).

# About Partnership Link-Up Service

PLUS seeks to bring together churches feeling the need of full-time help, and people who feel called by God to such ministry. It is neither a selecting nor an accrediting body.

Two confidential registers are maintained by the secretary, one of churches seeking help, the other of people willing to give such help.

The secretary and members of a panel of consultants, are willing to be consulted by churches and individuals.

The current secretary is **Alan Batchelor**, 15 Barncroft, Berkhamsted, Herts, HP4 3NL (Tel: 01442–864281), to whom all enquiries should be addressed.

# Introduction

## Alan Batchelor
### Secretary, Partnership Link-up Service

In the first half of the 1990s, there was considerable growth in the number of churches with 'Brethren' origins appointing a salaried worker, often on a full-time basis. Such fellowships were clearly not following the traditional pattern, but neither were they abandoning their biblical foundations. They were endeavouring to adapt to the pressures which modern life imposed on the church, and particularly the leadership. They believed that the vision was God-given, but were also aware that the practicalities of bringing it into reality were not to be treated lightly.

A small but growing number of such churches are discovering that there is both biblical warrant and practical need for the full-time ministry of women, as well as men, in local churches in UK. This has been done successfully in the overseas mission field.

It has always been recognised that this development would not be without hazards. There was a learning process for the churches, for their leaders, and for the new type of member, often described as a 'full-time worker'. Already, a considerable amount of experience has been gained, and problems have been more clearly identified over a wide range of relevant topics.

More often than not, workers were not to be found within the church membership, and a wider search was needed. The finding and introduction of an 'outsider' to a fellowship could give rise to a new range of complex issues.

Partnership Link-Up Service was established to provide a comprehensive resource for an identifiable type of church needing a worker, whether male or female, and for workers called by God and looking for appointments.

It was to provide a forum for sharing experience so far gained, and for discussing the issues that affected both church leaders and full-time workers that the consultation, 'Don't Muzzle the Ox', was held in July 1995. The chapters of this volume represent substantially the papers given at the consultation. After considering the basic concepts, much helpful advice is offered about appointing the worker—what really needs to be considered, and by whom.

On one side, it is recognised that the whole church fellowship—both leaders and members—need help and reassurance. Not all elderships have experience or knowledge of practical issues, such as the writing of a job description, the drafting of a contract and the formulation of a remuneration structure, acceptable to the Inland Revenue. Clearly, too, when a financially-supported full-time worker is introduced into the church, the church leaders will have to face a totally new regime. They will need to learn to work with the person appointed, making careful adjustments to old, possibly obsolete practices. The church members also, in addition to footing the bill, will need to be educated about the operation of an entirely new arrangement.

On the other side, the financially-supported worker's personal and family needs, his or her aspirations and resources, must be well thought through. They will probably be embarking on a new experience in which they will be learning 'on site', sorting out the priorities, using their gifts appropriately and, at the same time, trying to keep mentally, physically and spiritually on top of the job. The work might easily become a bottomless pit, and trying to cope with it could impose unmanageable pressures on the personal and family life of the worker.

There is no one incontrovertible solution which will apply to every fellowship. Since each situation is unique, no single model applies to each church or each worker. Nevertheless, these chapters will doubtless be of enormous help to elders and full-time workers going along this path, and will steer them past many of the pitfalls which others have discovered, sometimes at great cost. They will also provide an ongoing resource for fellowships which aim to operate harmonious, effective and spiritual churches, under the good hand of God.

# 1

# Principles and Practice

Neil Summerton
*Elder at Cholmeley Church, Highgate, London*

## FULL-TIME MINISTRY IN THE 'BRETHREN' TRADITION

The churches for whom this book is intended have, historically, some unique characteristics among Protestant churches in the last three centuries. Perhaps their most fundamental distinctive—in the proper sense of the word 'fundamental'—was a deeply radical rejection of the notion that any distinction of status should be drawn between Christian believers in the local church.

This thorough-going interpretation of the doctrine of the priesthood of all believers had a number of significant consequences which led to other distinctives. It contributed, for example, to the concept of an equality between believers in worship, in which all were free to participate, according to their various spiritual gifts, under the leadership of the Holy Spirit. It implied an equality with respect to authority so that, at the extreme, individual believers were not to be obliged to submit themselves to any human master in the church. The local community of believers was to be governed, if at all, by the (male) members as a whole, again under the direct authority of the Holy Spirit, rather than even by a group of elders.

It certainly implied that human training of itself, and still less an act of ordination, could not mark out any individual as having a special status, authority or position in the church. At best, these depended on the observed quality of the individual's actual ministry and the consequent blessing among believers and unbelievers. Hence, for example, if there were to be any elders at all, they were to be those whom the congregation accepted as already giving evidence of carrying out the necessary ministry.[1]

This body of what was perceived to be New Testament theory did not, of course, prevent the exercise of full-time ministry, made possible by the practical support of believers. 'Brethren' churches

---

[1]  See chapter 9 for a fuller discussion of 'Brethren' distinctives.

were outstanding, proportionately, for the scale of their full-time activity in foreign missions.[2] At home, there was no shortage of full-time evangelists, to whom may be attributed in considerable part the rapid expansion of congregations between 1860 and 1939. Nor did they lack itinerating Bible teachers, some of whom had very considerable influence in shaping the doctrine and culture of the body of churches as a whole.

But, despite the principle of commendation by a local congregation, all these full-time 'ministers' were particular in lacking any overt and direct cash nexus to an individual congregation or a denominational body. Virtually to a man and a woman, they worked on the 'faith principle' which the 'Brethren' fathers considered themselves to have discovered or rediscovered, and which they communicated to the whole evangelical movement in the second half of the nineteenth century.[3]

This factor itself had a number of consequences. First, it gave extensive freedom of decision to these full-time 'ministers' as to the location and nature of their ministry—and it almost certainly encouraged the individualism which they had in any case imbibed from the spirit of their times. It also reduced their authority and influence over individual congregations, if only because so very rarely were they securely based in any of them. The congregations themselves developed a tradition of doing without full-time input into their congregational life. This was probably a matter of practice to start with, but with time it became an article of doctrine that congregations should not enjoy, and did not need, full-time assistance.

The scale of input from congregational leaders in secular employment should not be under-estimated, however. Some could live comfortably on a limited number of hours each week. Both they, and other less well-to-do leaders, like Scottish colliers who taught themselves Hebrew and Greek to enhance their biblical understanding, thought nothing of giving the whole of their non-remunerated hours to furthering the life of their congregations. They did this without the benefit of any special status, beyond, perhaps, that of recognition as an elder—though this is not to denigrate the authority which they enjoyed by acclaim, or at least acquiescence, of the congregation. It came to be seen as the norm that the local congregation did not need full-time assistance, and could and should be led by people in secular employment.

---

[2] In the heyday, perhaps 1.5 -2.00% of the British Isles membership was engaged in overseas mission.

[3] See Klaus Fiedler, *The Story of Faith Missions*, Oxford: Regnum Lynx, 1994.

This theory of congregational leadership and full-time ministry became deeply ingrained in the 'Brethren' tradition. It lives on today in many 'Brethren', new 'Brethren', or former 'Brethren' leaders who are not in full-time ministry. At the same time, those leaders have often in the last twenty years seen the need to recruit full-time assistance for the local church. The evidence from other traditions (e.g., Anglican and Baptist) is that it is not always a straightforward matter to integrate a new full-time 'minister' into an established congregation, following an 'interregnum'.[4] But, given the special character of the 'Brethren' doctrine of ministry, and the strength with which it was held (often quite unconsciously), particular difficulty in absorbing paid full-time ministry into 'Brethren' and 'former Brethren' churches was wholly predictable[5] and has certainly been apparent in too many places.

The remainder of this contribution seeks to re-evaluate some of the issues in the light of scripture and the current situation in many of the local churches to which this volume is addressed. For greater details on the practical and relational difficulties, and the means of resolving them, the reader should refer to chapters 12–14 of the revised edition of *A Noble Task*.

## BIBLICAL FOUNDATIONS

The strength of the 'Brethren' tradition in these matters calls, in the first place, for some re-evaluation against the New Testament, which the tradition also takes to be the authoritative judge of tradition.

I start by summarising what I believe the New Testament teaches on this issue. It envisages financially-supported ministry (whether part-time or full-time) subsisting in the church alongside self-supported (full-time and part-time) ministry. The role, status and

---

[4]   For better or worse, the extra status of the full-time minister in those situations usually means that the discomforted church members seek fellowship elsewhere, or possible discontinue church involvement.

[5]   Chapter 8, 'Adapting to full-time congregational ministry' in *Servants of God: papers on the use of full-time workers in Brethren churches*', Exeter: The Paternoster Press for the Christian Brethren Research Fellowship, 1986, pp 85-94, sought to anticipate some of the difficulties. It was reprinted in slightly modified form in N W Summerton, *A Noble Task: eldership and ministry in the local church*, Exeter: Paternoster Press, 1987, pp 153–163 (revised edition, Carlisle: Paternoster Press, 1994, pp.173–183).

[6]   See footnote 5, above.

authority of each individual in the particular circumstances is determined by their gifts, rather than by notions of official status or the nature of and arrangements made for their financial support.

That the New Testament envisages full-time evangelistic and teaching ministry, dependent on the financial support of others, is so obvious that it scarcely needs demonstration. While the Lord himself received, as was normal for Jewish boys of his generation, a practical trade that would have enabled him to earn his living, his own itinerant ministry as a rabbi appears to have been full-time in character. Equally clearly, it depended on the support of others— frequently those to whom he was personally close (Mark 1:29–31; Luke 8:2,3; Matt 26:17–19; see also Matt 8:18–22). When sending out both the Twelve and the Seventy on their evangelistic and healing tours, he enjoined them, as a matter of principle, to make themselves dependent on others for their ministry—as much as anything as a test of the goodwill of those to whom they were sent (Luke 9:1–6; 10:1–12,18–20). Jesus justified this teaching specifically on the principle that 'the worker deserves his wages',[7] so much so that, curiously, he advised his disciples not to spread the burden among the potential hosts (Luke 10:7).

The apostle Paul appealed to the same principle in establishing, as a commandment from the Lord, the absolute right of apostles and 'those who preach the gospel' to 'receive their living from the gospel' (1 Cor 9:1–14). It is clear that Paul also assumed that those residing in the place where the evangelist and teacher was working had this duty of support, not simply those living elsewhere ('Who serves as a soldier at his own expense? Who plants a vineyard and does not eat of its grapes? Who tends a flock and does not drink of the milk?'-1 Cor 9:7). Incidentally, Paul made it plain that support of the apostles in their full-time ministry was the norm, and that his own practice was the exception: 'Don't we have the right to food and drink? Don't we have the right to take a believing wife along with us, as do the other apostles and the Lord's brothers and Cephas? Or is it only I and Barnabas who must work for a living?' (1 Cor:9:3–6). The same verses are explicit that the right and duty of support extend to the apostle's wife and, presumably, family.

Some years later, in his first letter to Timothy, Paul explicitly recognises that the right and duty of receiving and giving financial support extend to the (competent) elders of the local church, including, be it noted, those whose work is *not* teaching and preaching as well as, especially, those who have these ministries (1 Tim:5:17,18). Earlier in the chapter, he envisages regular financial

---

[7]   Biblical quotations are from the New International Version.

support for older widows who have an accepted pastoral and teaching ministry in the church—though he is clear that, where the widow's family can maintain such a widow-minister, they should do so, rather than allowing the burden to be placed upon the church at large (vv 3–11,16). At the very least, this leads to the conclusion that the duty of financial support in return for ministry beneficial to the church was not seen as reserved for a special class of apostles, priests, teachers or evangelists.

Paradoxically, the New Testament also unequivocally accepts self-supported ministry as a norm, though without in any way impairing the spiritual status and authority of the person concerned. Paul's farewell to the elders of Ephesus suggests that it was his normal practice to support himself and his team in their evangelistic and teaching ministry through his trade as a tent-maker (Acts 20:33–35). This seems also to have been the practice of his circle, including Priscilla and Aquila (Acts 18:3) and Barnabas, as already noted above, and although it must be a matter of speculation, it is hard to believe that his protégés like Timothy and Titus did not follow a similar practice.

For Paul, this was not simply a question of the practical consideration that, in pioneer evangelistic work, it was not possible to expect the nascent local church to support him. Nor was it a question of refusal to accept support from others as a matter of principle, for we have seen that Paul himself was unequivocal about his right to receive support from the church, and there are numerous references in his letters to his accepting support from churches elsewhere which he had founded (e.g., Phil 2:25). His preference had a two-fold purpose: to enable him to support the poor (Acts 20:35); and to make his message more effective as an aspect of making himself all things to all men for the sake of the gospel. He was anxious that unbelievers should not think that he was only in his ministry for what he could get out of it financially, so that they could discount what he had to say—a view which remains common enough today (1 Cor 9:15–27).

It is clear, too, that his preference had its cost—namely, that Christians and, possibly, the other apostles were inclined to think, as a result, that his ministry did not have the same authority as that of the other apostles, precisely because he and his team supported themselves. His express purpose in writing 1 Corinthians was to refute any such idea. His basis of financial support did *not* have the effect of making him a second-class apostle.

Consistent with this approach to the basis of Christian ministry in the local church, through the pages of the Acts of the Apostles and the apostolic letters we catch glimpses of individuals who have responsibilities outside the church but who occupy leadership positions within it. These may include Manaen (Acts 13:1) and certainly Erastus (Rom 16:23). It seems reasonable to suppose that, at least in the early days, many of those who were appointed elder in the infant churches continued in their earlier businesses and employments.

If the basis of financial support emphatically does not mark out some church leaders and ministers from others in biblical terms, perhaps we can look to some other ground of differentiation which gives a special status to some. Ordination, maybe?

In places, the New Testament locates authority in the Christian community as a whole (e.g., for the final decision in respect of excommunication and disputes between Christians—see Matt 18:17; 1 Cor 5:1–6:6). Elsewhere, authority is vested in apostles and elders in an official capacity (see, e.g., Acts 15:22,23;[8] 1 Cor 9:1,2; 2 Cor 1:23–2:4; 3:1–6; 12:11–13; 13:2,11; Philemon 8 for apostolic authority; and 1 Tim 3:4; 5:17; Tit 1:9,11, and 1 Pet 5:1–6, for the authority of elders). This authority and status, however, extends to *all* apostles and elders, rather than to some sub-class of them.

As for manual ordination, the practice is rather undeveloped and undefined in the New Testament documents. The laying on of hands appears to have been extensively used for a variety of purposes. These include healing (e.g., Acts 9:17), for initial conferment of the Holy Spirit on new believers (Acts 8:17), to commend individuals to a specific spiritual mission (Acts 13:3), to appoint to a specific task of an official kind (Acts 6:6) and to confer what appears to have been a specific spiritual gift or gifts (1 Tim 4:13,14; 2 Tim 1:4[9]). Interestingly, scripture is silent as to whether Paul and Barnabas laid on hands in appointing elders (Acts 14:23), though there is sufficient evidence to enable us reasonably to infer that it became normal in appointing elders. This evidence includes the action of the apostles in appointing the Seven (Acts 6:1–6), the parallel with Paul and Barnabas's own commendation in Acts 13:3, and the action of the elders in conferring gift on Timothy.

---

[8]   Though, even in this case, the text is clear that the apostles and elders acted 'with the whole church' (v22).

[9]   It does not seem absolutely certain that Paul is referring to the same incident in these two scriptures. In the first, the laying on of hands is said to be by the body of elders, and in the second to be by Paul himself. In the latter case, he might be referring to initial conferment of the Holy Spirit on Timothy's first confession of faith.

But, in relation to the laying on of hands, the focus of the New Testament is on the conferment of gift, rather than the identification of special status within the church or its hierarchy as such. And, in any case, the laying on of hands in the New Testament is no more than a recognition of the spiritual reality, namely the gift and ministry conferred directly by God himself and evidenced in the subsequent achievements of the ministry concerned (see 1 and 2 Cor as a whole, and, especially, 2 Cor 3:1–6).

We cannot identify anything broadly analogous to ordination, at least as understood in either the Orthodox and Catholic traditions in relation to the priesthood, or the Nonconformist tradition in relation to the pastorate. That is a post-biblical development. Insofar as manual ordination should be seen as conferring special official status in the church, it is probably better to see it as conferring that status upon *all* elders and deacons, rather than upon some sub-class of them. The burden of the New Testament is that the right to minister in a particular manner derives not from status, but from spiritual gift, the proportion in which it is enjoyed by the individual concerned, and that individual's willingness to exercise it (see, in addition to the scriptures already cited, Rom 12:3–6; 1 Cor 12,14; Eph 4:7–16).

## IMPLICATIONS FOR 'BRETHREN' CHURCHES APPOINTING FULL-TIME WORKERS

From this summary, some deductions can reasonably be drawn which bring us a little closer to the practical situation facing many local churches of 'Brethren' background as they grapple with the issues presented by the development of appointing full-time elders and other full-time workers. They are principles which, if observed, will, I believe, assist in resolving some of the difficulties and tensions that are being encountered as a result.

*First,* and contrary to the received truth in many 'Brethren' circles, there *is absolutely no reason of biblical principle to bar 'full-time' ministries from established local churches. (Though it might be less misleading, both to the workers concerned and to the congregations, if we were to think of*

---

[10] I do not, of course, mean to imply in any way that God does not frequently abundantly bless the ministry of those who have been so ordained. So far as Nonconformist ordination is concerned, I think greater weight is placed on the passages in 1 and 2 Timothy than they will bear in the light of the New Testament as a whole, and that many Nonconformist Bible colleges need to reconsider what they convey to students on this point.

*them as being 'financially-supported' ministries—to distinguish them from 'self-supported' ministries.)*

The early church grew and flourished, in part because of the dedicated ministry of financially-supported apostles, their assistants, and elders. That has been so throughout the history of the church. It was so in the growth stages of the 'Brethren' movement—though this was masked by the extent of the commitment to the 'faith principle' of financial support. There is reason to think that financially-supported elders and other workers have a massive contribution to make today. This is being borne out by what is happening in many local churches that are making use of financially-supported ministries.

**Second,** *the mix of financially-supported and self-supported ministries can be expected to vary from time to time and from place to place. The scope for either can be restricted unreasonably by doctrinal principle, as we have already seen. It should not be. But it is entirely legitimate for the mix to be determined by practical considerations.*

It may be that the opportunities and burdens make it essential to support people in ministry if the Lord is to be honoured in the work. It may be that the demands of pastoral care and of the needy are greater now than they were. It may be that the pressures on the self-supported, compared with earlier years, are such that they cannot make the time available to carry out the work of the church competently, so that assistance from financially-supported workers is essential. All these factors may point to greater use of the financially-supported.

At the same time, however, it is worth noting that working hours are shorter than ever was the case in the past, that holiday allowances are longer, that working 'lives' are shortening dramatically, and therefore that opportunities for Christian ministry by the young before employment begins, and by the retired (who enjoy longer and healthier lives) are a major resource for the church. Coupled with greater educational atttainment than in former generations, these factors should mean that moves within Evangelicalism and Christendom generally to enable the people of God to exercise its gifts, rather than relying on those of a clerical group, are working with the practical grain of the times.

In our consumerist society, the question does often arise, however, whether in many churches there is the same level of commitment to Christian work that marked former generations, and whether the claims of personal leisure, recreation and travel do not often take priority. A modern application of taking up one's cross may be precisely in this area.

And it may be, too, that one of the key roles of full-time elders and other financially-supported workers is, in preference to doing the work themselves, to mobilise the vast pool of gift that is locked up in the self-supported in the church. It remains a question whether the training of the financially-supported is yet sufficiently well-adjusted to ensure that they see themselves more as behind-the-scenes enablers and coordinators, than always as up-front doers. (Sometimes the self-supported are better at this enabling role because it is the mode of leadership that they trained to adopt in their secular lives.)

*Third, the significance, role and status of an individual should not be determined by whether or not the individual is financially-supported by the church, or by whether they have been subject to some form of ordination, or by whether they have received some form of theological or pastoral training (though the last factor may well be relevant to the practical competence and effectiveness with which they exercise their spiritual gifts). Nor, however, should they be determined by the reverse of these considerations.*

It does not follow that the financially-supported worker should, of necessity, be the top leader in a local church—or, on the other hand, that they should always be subordinate to the elders. If financially-supported workers possess spiritual gifts and calibre of a high order, it is nonsense to suggest that they should be subordinate to a group of possibly incompetent self-supported elders—though such individuals should submit to the disciplines and benefits of group leadership. (The New Testament accounts leave room for inferring that, on occasion, both Peter and Paul would have done well to listen more to the wisdom of their brethren!) On the other hand, it may frequently be the case that the person best suited to be the 'leader of the leaders' is someone who happens to be called to remain in secular employment.

To put it bluntly, who leads and who leads the leaders should be determined by gift and experience, not by status or the manner of their support. If, however, the key leadership roles fall to the self-supported, they will have to be prepared to give the necessary priority of time and effort to the task, and make the necessary self-sacrifices that are demanded.

It is in this area that, in my judgment, many of the difficulties are arising. Partly, it is a question of the expectations of the financially-supported workers, and their perceptions (consciously or subconsciously) of the status that they ought, as a matter of course, to be accorded. Partly, it is a question of the expectations of congregations.

The attitude and training of the financially-supported often leads them to assume that they must be 'boss' in the local church. The concept of leadership that is customary in churches of 'Brethren' background often seems not to be understood by them, and to be rejected if it is. Congregations may have a similar assumption, because that is the model of church leadership with which they are familiar from both history and society around them. This is also reinforced by the trend towards professionalism in Western society. The paid staff worker is assumed to be the king-pin, to the detriment of unpaid input, a phenomenon which has been noted in secular as well as religious voluntary associations. These assumptions are further reinforced by the greater practical accessibility of the full-time person, a perfectly legitimate reason for according precedence to such a person.

Elders and some congregational members, however, drawing on a quite different tradition, often imagine that nothing will change with the introduction of a financially-supported full-time worker. Particularly if the worker is younger, they see the person as inevitably subordinate to the elders—at the extreme as a dogsbody who will do the work and ensure growth without threatening their power or leadership or the existing dynamics of the leadership group. It is this attitude of mind that often leads churches of 'Brethren' background to appoint younger financially-supported workers. It is reinforced by the belief that the reason for decline is ineffective evangelism, and that therefore what is needed is an evangelist or youth worker. In fact, the prior condition of evangelistic effectiveness is a spiritual renewal of congregational life, and such renewal requires senior input by pastor-teachers/leaders. But the existing leadership is unwilling to contemplate the change in leadership dynamics which would result.

These two contrary assumptions, on top of normal human relational difficulties (which tend to be magnified in small unstructured voluntary associations—secular as well as religious), all too frequently make for explosive results, which are deeply distressing, both for the congregations and the full-time workers concerned.

*Fourth, in today's conditions, there is a wide variety of tasks that financially-supported workers can shoulder, full-time or part-time, in the local church. The place of the individual in the leadership of the church may therefore vary with their age, the nature of the task, and their particular gifts and capacity. It is perfectly reasonable that it should do so.*

As discussed at greater length in *A Noble Task*, and in chapter 8 below, there are all sorts of tasks that may need to be borne in the local church, and which might well be filled by a financially-supported worker. Those of pastor, pastor-teacher, coordinator/administrator, evangelist, worship leader, youth worker, community worker, and social worker spring to mind in a list that is by no means exhaustive.

It is evident that these different tasks will permit differing relationships with the leadership group of the church. It will probably be essential that anyone carrying out the first four or five of these tasks will need a particularly close relationship with the eldership, since they are very much the task of the elder, and the financially-supported worker should be seen by the congregation as marching absolutely in step with the eldership. Churches should, in my judgment, beware of appointing people to such roles without making them elders.

It may not be essential for the remaining tasks to be carried out by an elder, but there should nevertheless be a good relationship and understanding with the eldership, and good supervision. There are too many cases in which young financially-supported workers appear to have been left with virtually no moral support from church leaderships. When that occurs, it is not surprising if the supported worker becomes cynical and disrespectful about the capacity of the leaders.

*Fifth,* careful thought should be given to the basis of the financial arrangement between a congregation and a supported worker.

Though, in the light of the scriptural analysis above, the question of financial support should not be determinative, the reality is that, for the reasons already discussed, it does seem to influence perceptions and attitudes in ways that seem to me to be unhelpful.

There cannot be any biblical argument against paying a supported worker a fixed salary on the basis of a contract, with accommodation provided etc. That will be the expectation of many prospective supported workers. And the arrangement has the advantage of shifting responsibiity to the elders and the congregation. Under such an arrangement, it is the appointers, rather than the appointee, who have to live by faith!

But the arrangement does have the effect of emphasising the differentiation of the supported worker from the rest of the workers within the congregation. Why, it may be asked, should the financially-supported worker, as a concomitant of his or her contract, be the only person within the congregation who has a job description, performance targets etc? At the very least, some of the self-supported leaders might do a better job if *they* had job descriptions, too!

Here the tradition of living by faith may have some relevance. It may be that if the financially-supported worker does not have a specific cash nexus with the congregation, set out in a contract, the conflicts of attitude with which I have wrestled above will be less acute, and less violence will be done to the concepts of group leadership and multiple exercise of gift in the local church. (These I hold to be important insights contributed by the 'Brethren' movement.)

That approach has its risks, of course, not least the temptation to individualism and rejection of personal accountability on the part of the worker, and the (greater) temptation to the congregation to neglect its financial obligations to the worker 'living by faith' in their midst. Thanks to housing laws in the UK, it also has legal consequences where accommodation is provided by the congregation (a service tenancy requires the existence of a contract of employment). But the arrangement is worth considering in the 'Brethren' and 'post-Brethren' setting. My observation is that full-time leadership has been most successfully integrated where it has been based on that principle.

## CONCLUSION

None of this is meant to discourage the integration of financially-supported leadership in 'Brethren' and 'post-Brethren' churches. As has been said, that has absolute biblical sanction, and it would be folly, for which those responsible would in due course be accountable, to deny the church such leadership where that is God's will. But the rights and opportunities of self-supported leaders need protecting today, just as much as they did in New Testament times. And it would be a pity if, just when the principles of group leadership and multiple exercise of gift are being applied widely in the Christian church, those in the 'Brethren' tradition were to revert to an old-fashioned and, in my view, unbiblical form of monarchical leadership of the local church.

# 2

# Selection and Appointment

Alex McIlhinney
*Elder at York Community Church,*
*and*
Norman Murray
*Elder at Salway Evangelical Church, Woodford Green, Essex.*

## INTRODUCTION

The term 'financially-supported worker' (FSW) is here adopted as it seems to be the most appropriate and accurate term to describe those who work, usually, but not necessarily, full-time, in our churches. The term 'full-time worker', which has come into fairly widespread use, is less than satisfactory since it does not distinguish FTWs from unpaid voluntary workers. Nor, for that matter, does it describe the variety of workers and arrangements found in practice.

The FSWs found most commonly in our churches can broadly be categorised as pastors, youth workers and community workers. Neil Summerton's contribution later in this volume (chapter 8) discusses their roles. All are in mind in this chapter, though some points made apply mainly to pastors.

Careful planning and investigation, together with the relevant professional advice, are vital if the matters here discussed are to be conducted correctly and honourably between church and FSW. The days when practical issues, such as finance, housing and transport could be addressed on an informal and ad hoc basis by a few individuals are long gone. One reason for this is that the state has introduced legislation governing the relationship between employer and employee, and if the church decides to take this path it has no choice but to conform to that legislation. Churches dare not be offhand, or less than wholly scrupulous, in discharging duties and responsibilities to the FSW and to the various authorities.

It should be recognised, even when grappling with the detail of regulations, that the purpose of ensuring all things are done 'decently and in order' is to free both FSW and those to whom he or she is directly responsible, to concentrate as much as possible upon the spiritual goals towards which the church is striving through the FSW's appointment.

The following matters demand serious prior commitment by the parties involved.

## JOB DESCRIPTION

### ESTABLISH THE NEED

An increasing number of 'Brethren' churches have found it necessary to have one or more FSWs because of a combination of two main factors: the change in culture resulting in greatly increased secular work demands; and the realisation that fear lest such an appointment should lead to monarchical leadership is seldom justified.

Misguided reasons for seeking a FSW which are seldom articulated but, nevertheless, have often been present, include the following: it might somehow halt the decline in church membership; it will automatically solve all, or at least some, of the problems currently facing the church; it will make life easier for the existing leaders who are feeling the strain of leadership; it must be right for this church since others are doing it and seem to be benefiting from it.

More commendable reasons for seeking a FSW include the following: to enable the church to realise more adequately its outreach potential; to encourage the development of the gifts of church members; to make available more time to identify a vision and a strategy for the church; to provide better and more consistent teaching and preaching; to improve the nurture and pastoral care of members and contacts.

Before seeking to find and appoint a FSW, certain preliminary actions are essential, in addition to much prayer and waiting upon the Lord–nothing in what follows should be taken to minimise the importance of this.

First, the church leadership should assess, as honestly and thoroughly as possible, the strengths and weaknesses of the church and any opportunities or threats facing it. In this process, church members should be consulted as much as possible. The church leadership should then seek to identify the main areas of need, and to assess the importance and priority of each. Next, it will be necessary to perform a careful analysis of the tasks which it is thought a FSW could carry out to the benefit of the whole church.

In doing so, they must have arrived at certain conclusions about the desired direction and development of the medium term—say 4–6 years hence—and assessed how far these goals are attainable, given the present gifts available in the church. One would expect the conclusion to have been reached that some important tasks cannot be carried on at all, or only partially, from lack of available or effective gift. Alternatively, it may be anticipated that an aspect of the work which is established and shows potential for further growth would be hampered without the additional gift being utilised. In practice, a mixture of both situations will often be found.

The church as a whole needs to face up to the practical and financial consequences of appointing a FSW. If there is a conviction that this action is right, it may only be necessary for all the church members to increase their giving to a realistic level, based on scriptural principles, to meet this extra cost. If the church does not feel able to provide adequate financial support for a FSW it should seek another way of meeting its needs.

The church leadership needs to prepare the membership for the changes which the appointment of a FSW will inevitably bring, by clear teaching, open discussion and good communication. Incidentally, but importantly, those changes will include adjustments to the individual roles of existing church leaders.

## DEFINE THE ROLE

The most important point, here, is that there is no one model, and certainly not an all-embracing word, to describe the role the FSW is to play. In particular, it is unlikely that churches seeking to appoint a FSW for the first time will want a 'minister' or 'pastor' such as commonly found in other nonconformist churches. There is therefore no substitute for choosing words which clearly but concisely define the role of the FSW. If a term is used (e.g., 'pastor') which has a particular connotation in the wider Christian church, then all church members must be certain what is envisaged by its use in their local context.

In any event, if the worker is an employee, a job title is required under the Employment Protection (Consolidation) Act 1978 (see the section below on 'Contracts/terms and conditions'). It goes without saying, however, that the precise title is much less important than the job which will be done.

## DRAW UP A JOB DESCRIPTION

The analysis of the need described above may well have revealed that what the church needs is an omnicompetent, multi-talented individual, blessed with all the spiritual gifts imaginable. If so, plan B should be adopted! Rarely will any one FSW be able to discharge more than three specific roles effectively (from those of pastoral worker, teacher, evangelist, administrator, youth worker etc). On the other hand, most suitable candidates will probably be able to fulfil at least two of the envisaged roles satisfactorily.

It is for the elders to select the overriding priority or priorities among the tasks identified, and to ensure that the appointed person is well able to drive forward the vital strategic goals in these areas. It is also evident that any attempt to mould the individual to fit a role for which he or she is unsuited (or even a pious hope that the FSW will somehow 'grow' into it) is a recipe for failure.

In any event, there should be a list of the tasks which the FSW is expected to perform, with sufficient detail to leave no doubt as to the priorities and objectives. This must, of course, be drawn up well before the first purposeful discussion with the candidate, and will be of enormous help in clarifying and anchoring the role in the minds of church leaders and members.

Provision should likewise be made for the job description to be reviewed, at least annually, though not too frequently, and adjusted as appropriate in the light of experience in the job.

If a church has previously had a FSW, it is still advisable to repeat most of these steps for a further appointment. The needs of a church change over time, and the job description will need to be adjusted to reflect the latest assessment of the situation and needs

## RECRUITMENT AND SELECTION

From the beginning of the process of recruitment and selection, the church leaders should remind themselves of the need to be realistic in their expectations, although obviously seeking the best man or woman. While keeping clearly in mind the main requirements and not compromising on these, if there is a real conviction that a particular applicant is 'right' and meets at least the most important needs of the church, there should be a readiness to amend the job description to match the particular strengths and gifts of the individual. Patience and perseverance may be necessary, and the temptation to appoint 'the best of the bunch' should be avoided.

The sources from which applicants can be obtained include the following:

- Personal contacts of church leaders or individuals known to a church member. This is often the best source and should be pursued first.

- Partnership Link Up Service (PLUS), a Partnership service currently run by Alan Batchelor (15 Barncroft, Berkhamsted, Herts, HP4 3NL. Tel: 01442 864281).
- Dovetail, a somewhat similar service which provides workers from a much wider churchmanship. Contact Geoff Thompson, Christian Vocations, Holloway Street West, Lower Gornal, Dudley, West Midlands, DY3 2DZ (Tel: 01902 882836).
- Advertisements may be placed in Christian magazines such as *Christianity* and *Evangelicals Now*.
- Bible colleges. These may be approached direct, and will put advertisements on their notice boards. It is wise to think about the most appropriate time in relation to college terms and the academic year, bearing in mind that students will be looking for placements soon after the January of their final academic year. This source is suitable for more than youth workers, since, these days, there are many mature students, some already possessing pastoral experience.

The process of appointing a FSW will vary according to the experience of the members of the church leadership and the way in which the church is accustomed to make major decisions. It may well include the following.

- *Initial interview* In preparation for this, the applicant should be provided with three documents: a profile of the church giving the information about the church that the applicant needs to know (this will save valuable time at the interview); a provisional job description; and a detailed application form. [See appendix 1] If there are numerous applicants, interviews may well be handled by two of the leadership, preferably the same two for all interviews, to ensure consistency.
- *Interview of short-listed applicants* This should involve all the leaders and the spouse of the applicant.
- *Visit of applicant*, with spouse, at least once, to the church for a Sunday without any public involvement.
- *Applicant to preach at church*, at least once, if this is to be an important part of the envisaged role.
- *Take up references* If a reference is to be really helpful it is advisable to send a detailed reference request containing the questions to which you want answers. [See appendix 2] A telephone conversation with the person giving the reference can also be valuable.
- *A meeting of church members* should be arranged, at which the applicant can present to the church his or her calling and vision, and answer questions put by any church mem-

ber. Further discussion and questions addressed to the
church leadership can follow, in the absence of the applicant.

- *The final decision* should be taken by the church leaders, or
by the membership, according to the church's agreed procedure for taking major decisions. It is usually wise to allow
time to elapse between the meeting of the applicant with the
church members and the taking of the final decision, in order
to allow further consideration and comments from church
members before the decision is made. This allows time for
reflection and enables the minority who do not find it easy to
express their concerns publicly to do so privately to the
church leaders.

## CONTRACT/ TERMS AND CONDITIONS

It is highly desirable, if not essential, to have a signed contract
including all the main elements of the arrangements made. This
should go a long way towards avoiding the misunderstandings
which can so easily emerge in the course of time and sour relationships at a later stage.

Whether a FSW is an employee, or self-employed, can sometimes be a difficult question (for fuller discussion, see section on
'Taxation . . .', below). It is not simply a matter of choosing what
is preferred. It follows from the nature of the arrangements as set
out in the contract, and how these work out in practice. The Inland
Revenue (IR) will often seek to establish employed status because
it suits them better, and because most Inspectors do not understand the genuine plurality of leadership in our churches. In many
cases, however, the right interpretation of the arrangement is self-employment, and this should be vigorously argued if it is the case.

There are a number of indicators of self-employment, the most
important of which is whether the FSW is subject to the 'control'
of the church leadership. If this is the case, the FSW is an employee.
If, however, the FSW has substantial freedom as to how and when
the work within the agreed arrangements in the contract and the
spiritual considerations of accountability in common with all
church members is done, then the FSW may well be self-employed.

If the FSW is an employee, then a clear statement of the terms
and conditions of service is essential, both by law, and as a matter
of courtesy and good practice. Even if the FSW is self-employed,
several of the matters dealt with below in the section on taxation,
will still need to be addressed and, again as good practice, agreed
in writing between the parties. One must, however, take care not
to include any matters which are exclusively applicable to

employees, lest the dividing line between employment and self-employment should appear inadvertently to have been crossed.

Employment law in UK is complicated and, partly under the influence of directives from the European Commmission, is constantly changing—a fact which any church leader with employer responsibilities in secular life will readily acknowledge. Even where some experience of staff employment resides within the appointing group, professional advice is often essential.

Employees are entitled to certain minimum rights under the Employment Protection (Consolidation) Act 1978 (EPCA 78) which can serve as a basic model. As suggested later, however, more than the legal minimum requirements should be met for FSWs.

## CONTRACT

EPCA 78 places an obligation upon the employer to provide the employee with a written statement of conditions of service within 13 weeks of commencing employment. Although this statement is not in itself a contract, it can in effect become one if the employee signifies that he or she accepts it as a true record of the agreed contract.

## TERMS AND CONDITIONS

The statement of conditions referred to above must cover the following matters:

### The parties

Precisely who the employer is can be a matter of debate (again, see section on 'Taxation . . .', below). For a number of reasons, it is considered that the church itself, or at least the church council within it, should be the employer.

### The date when employment began

### Job title

The act does not require a job description to be included, but, as discussed above, there are obvious advantages in doing this.

### Pay

The rate of pay, when and how it will be paid, and what provisions there are for reviewing pay if the employment is for longer than one year, must be included.

*Hours of work*

*Entitlement to holidays, including public holidays, and holiday pay.*

*Sickness and sick pay*

Unless this is specifically excluded, an employee is entitled to sick pay, and schemes to deal with this often cover matters such as minimum service qualification, production of medical certificates, self certification, contributory insurance schemes.

*Pensions and pension schemes*

It is not compulsory that the employer should provide a pension for the employee, although clearly the level of financial support should be such as to enable pension contributions to be made (if self-employed by means of a personal pension). The earlier in life that pension contributions commence, the better. Whatever it is, the position must be stated. (See below, under 'Other issues' for a discussion of the technical aspects.)

*Termination provisions (both sides)*

The Act provides for a minimum of one week for the first two years of employment and one week per year thereafter up to a maximum of 12. This is clearly inadequate, and a period of several months (3–6) is much preferable.

*Grievance procedures*

A procedure must be laid down to achieve a resolution, should grievance arise. In the normal run of events, this will make clear to whom the individual is answerable.

A contract for the provision of services by a self-employed individual should cover similar matters in an appropriately modified way.

OTHER TERMS AND CONDITIONS

In addition to these required conditions in a contract of employment, it would be wise also to make some provision for the following (in the contract or in some other form):

*Status*

What is the FSW's status within the church structure, especially in regard to the elders or other leadership group? If, as is so often the case, the FSW is to act as an elder, then this should be stated.

*Areas of work*

It is advisable to set out in some detail the extent of involvement agreed, such as the time to be given to vision and strategy, the proportion of teaching and preaching at main services, the extent of involvement in pastoral care and in what way.

*Accountability and consultation*

There should be a clear understanding about the degree of personal authority and the expectation about consultation.

*Accommodation*

It is normally much more satisfactory for the FSW to own his or her own home, and to receive financial support at such a level as to enable the mortgage repayments on it to be met. This means that, when the appointment with the church ends, the FSW is not left without a home as well as a job. (The technical aspects of providing accommodation will be discussed below, under 'Other issues'.)

*Church office*

It is usually better for the FSW to have an office other than at home, for the sake of the family.

*Role of spouse*

This should be fully discussed at the appointment stage in order to avoid misunderstandings and unfair expectations. The spouse should be free to use gifts and have a job, just like any other church member.

*Pastoring*

The FSW, who will probably be doing a great deal of pastoring, also needs to receive pastoring. This should probably come primarily from the church leadership, but there is also great value in a properly established arrangement for regular pastoring from a trusted leader outside of the church.

*Period of the appointment*

It is helpful to state the length of time envisaged for the appointment, whilst recognising that this should not be expected to be applied rigidly.

*Training and personal development*

The FSW should be encouraged and helped to take time each year for appropriate training courses, attendance at conferences and private study. How this is to be arranged should probably be covered.

*Review of the past and plans for the future*

In a healthy relationship, this will be a continuous process but, in any event, at regular intervals there needs to be a more formal review of progress in the tasks set out in the job description, and a making of plans for the future.

## TAXATION AND RELATED MATTERS

Many difficulties are encountered in this area.

### EMPLOYER

As indicated briefly above, identifying the employer can be more difficult than at first imagined. Many churches will have an anti-quated trust deed which was probably set up to establish legal ownership of land and buildings. Some of these deeds will not contain a power to employ staff, and so an amendment to include this may be necessary.

A more modern constitution, such as one registered with the Charity Commissioners relatively recently, will almost certainly provide that the administration of the church will be in the hands of a council of management, and typically they will be able to employ. Some churches may have both trustees and a council of management. Provided these bodies are content to let the day to day relationship with the FSW reside with the elders (or a small group of elders) no great harm may be done in practice. The usual experience is that, when registering with the local IR office as an employer, the officials are content to accept 'X Church' as the employer, without further enquiry.

Other, sadder, experience would nevertheless teach that, over a period, the trustees on the one hand and the elders or leadership group on the other may diverge in both personnel and strategic aim. For this reason, if possible, the church, represented in practice by the treasurer (who is responsible to the elders) should be recorded as the employer.

### FSW—EMPLOYEE OR SELF-EMPLOYED?

Whether or not an individual is an employee or a self-employed person, is critical in the determination of rights and obligations in taxation, National Insurance Contributions (NICs), health and safety, sick and redundancy pay and maternity rights. In addition, third parties, such as insurance companies, may need to ascertain status in relation to liability to injury. It is therefore important that the agreement between church and FSW is comprehensive and unambiguous. Failure to make the correct deductions or pay the appropriate contributions can lead to recovery proceedings for several back years.

The IR has published a booklet (IR56) entitled 'Employed or Self Employed?' This is a helpful, but certainly not comprehensive guide to the factors to be taken into account in deciding whether a person is an employee or a self-employed person. Other useful publications include 'The Employers Guide to PAYE' (P7) and 'The Employers Guide to NI Contributions' (NP15).

## PRELIMINARY WARNINGS

- Most tax allowances and rates change annually, as do state benefits and NICs.
- The notes which follow cannot possibly be anything like comprehensive, and again, the importance of enlisting professional help, where necessary, must be emphasised.
- In recent years, the Revenue has become rather more aggressive in its audit of PAYE matters, and the yield from these enquiries has risen. Small employers, such as churches with only one, or at most a handful of employees, are unlikely to feature near the top of a hit list. Be that as it may, the reclassification as employees of people previously masquerading as self-employed workers is a popular and fruitful area. In addition, different local offices need not take the same attitude to a given set of circumstances, and it is therefore impossible to generalise.

## THE EMPLOYEE WORKER

The employer has a statutory obligation to deduct income tax under PAYE rules, and to account for it to the Collector of Taxes; and to ensure that Class 1 NICs are also paid by both employer and employee to the Collector.

Tax under Schedule E is charged on the 'emoluments' of an office of employment, including 'all salaries, fees, wages, perquisites and profits whatsoever'. Lest any doubts should remain, where inclusive earnings are £8,500 or above, further legislation ensures that virtually every benefit in kind, whether convertible to cash or not, is also assessable to tax. It seems reasonable that the FSW (if male) should earn at least the average of all male workers or perhaps, as some have decided, the average of the incomes of all members in the church who are in employment. If so, it will follow that the FSW's earnings, which for this purpose include benefits, will clearly exceed the absurdly static limit of £8,500 (unchanged since 1979) above which the FSW becomes a 'higher paid employee' (sic).

Benefits in kind, often referred to as 'fringe benefits' include, for example, the provision of a car and petrol, a loan at a reduced or nil rate of interest, accommodation, payment of mortgage interest, and many others. A return of benefits must be made annually to the Revenue by the employer on form P11D, and by the employee in his or her tax return. IR booklet 480 gives guidance.

An employee is entitled to deduct from these amounts any expenses which are 'wholly necessarily, and exclusively' incurred in the performance of his or her duties—words which are notoriously rigid and restricted in their operation (and in contrast to the more liberal allowance of expenses to the self-employed). In practice, the business proportion of expenditure will be allowable. Some relief should be available for a room in the home set aside for study/counselling; but the cost of home to work travel is not allowable, nor would be the purchase of most books and journals (or the Partnership subscription!). The Revenue will need to be persuaded of the reasonableness of amounts claimed.

So far as car expenses are concerned, it is worth noting that, if the church has agreed with the IR to operate a 'Fixed Profit Car Scheme', the amount of tax relief will depend upon the mileage covered and the size of the car's engine. The relief is much higher for the first 4,000 miles per annum. (This is dealt with in the section 'Other issues', below.)

A final, very important point is that, with effect from the 1996–97 tax year, a new system of self-assessment has been introduced for employees as well as for self-employed persons. For most people, this will commence with the income tax return issued on or around 6 April 1997 to cover income for the previous year and expenses of the year commencing upon that date. Not all employees will receive one, but the broad thrust of the change is intended to ensure that each taxpayer under the new system will deal with only one local office and receive only one tax bill for all income. Taxpayers will be encouraged to take a greater responsibility for working out their own tax bills, although the full details of this are beyond the scope of this chapter.

Other points which might arise include:

- The FSW's freedom (need?) to earn elsewhere. The status of this money can be difficult to determine. If the sums received more than cover the expenses of the assignment, then the total amount should be declared, together with an expenses claim. In some cases, this may amount to a separate source of income.

- Gifts other than salary. These are taxable if they arise out of the employment, but not if given in a personal capacity. This is a fine distinction, and if such gifts are given by the employing church, the IR may try to argue that these are further earnings from the employment and, therefore, fully taxable. On the other hand, it may be shown to the Inspector's satisfaction that additional amounts received are genuine gifts made, for example, at birthdays, Christmas, or to help with holidays, in a way which might arise for other friends or colleagues.

## THE SELF-EMPLOYED WORKER

The self-employed person in a profession or vocation is not subject to PAYE, but instead pays tax directly to the Collector of Taxes in January and July annually. Again, the system is in the throes of change, as a result, in part, of the new self-assessment regime referred to earlier. In addition, the considerable delay between earning of income and payment of tax which self-employed persons have typically enjoyed in the past will be greatly reduced by the new system. (Again, the details are complex, and further advice should be taken.)

An important point to note under the new rules is that, with effect from the 1997 return, a self-employed person will be legally required to keep records for 5 years from the 31 January following the end of the tax year concerned, with a penalty of £3,000 maximum upon failing to do this.

On the other hand, life can be simpler for people earning less than £15,000 (gross) a year, in which case there is no need to produce full blown accounts to the Tax Inspector—a three line account showing income, expenses and net profit will suffice. This, however, does not reduce the amount of record keeping required, as the self-employed must be able to substantiate the accounts, in case the Inspector wishes to look at the detail.

As regards expenses, the 'necessarily' test does not apply and, since the self-employed can claim expenses 'wholly and exclusively laid out or expended for the purposes of the profession or vocation', this gives a far greater scope than is enjoyed by the employee. Again, where there is a private element (e.g., car, telephone, study etc) an apportionment will be agreed. Allowances for depreciation on some capital assets, such as a motor car, may be claimed.

The total earnings of the FSW's spouse are tax free up to £4,045 (in 1997–98), although NIC will be payable. Wages paid by the

FSW to his or her partner can be claimed as an expense, provided these can genuinely be justified by the duties carried out. Reasonable remuneration should not be difficult to substantiate.

Class 2 and Class 4 NICs are due from the self-employed. In 1997–98, these will amount at the most to some £1,350. (By contrast, the employer's and employee's Class 1 contributions would together amount to over £2,300 in 1997–98 on a salary of £17,000.) One half of Class 4 NICs are no longer deductible for tax purposes.

There are, however, consequences which flow from self-employed status, and these should be weighed carefully alongside the financial benefits.

- Self-employed do not come within the ambit of EPCA 78, and thus have no statutory rights as regards, for example, sick pay. Fewer state benefits are available.
- Pension provision is the responsibility of the individual.
- For the self-employed FSW (although not for the church or churches among whom he or she will work) there is a significantly greater burden of record keeping. A simple cash book, recording all receipts and payments, should normally suffice, together with the appropriate receipts, provided the book is kept scrupulously up to date (i.e., not written up every other week).

As with the employed FSW, some uncertainty can arise over the status of sums received in a personal capacity. It is particularly important that the source of 'private' money should be recorded, in case a query arises later on.

GENERAL CONSIDERATIONS

Many people feel that the administrative burdens and strict rules inherent in the PAYE system are onerous, and favour the self-employed route. On the other hand, there is some measure of certainty and immediacy which may be welcome. In other respects, though, the balance of advantage will lie the other way. It should, however, be noted that it is not simply a question of just 'going' self-employed, for there has to be sufficient evidence to convince the Inspector that this is the correct status. The message, therefore, is clear: the contract must be meticulously thought out in advance, with input from both sides and preferably also from someone professionally engaged in a relevant discipline.

Overall, though, it may be suggested that, provided proper care is taken over non-fiscal matters, the self-employed route is preferable, if it can be justified. In many cases, this may accord with reality, since seldom in a church/FSW relationship will there exist the measure of detailed control over the way tasks are carried out to establish a truly master-servant position. On the other hand, in a number of cases it may be clear that this really is the truth of the matter, and if this is so, then of course the consequences must be fully accepted, and the authorities notified accordingly.

The presence of non-fiscal factors may well sway the decision, and cause arrangements to be skewed in a particular direction. For example, some church leaders and FSWs feel that self-employed status leads to an easier relationship between FSW and elders or other employing group. This may, in turn, partly depend upon whether the FSW is a member of the employing body. He or she is certainly unlikely to be a trustee, and would probably also be prohibited from serving on the council of management, if in receipt of a regular income from the church. Experience suggests that, even if the FSW is an employee, matters fiscal and financial need cause no embarrassment if they are the responsibility of a small group composed of one (or at most two) of the elders, together with the treasurer and (say) two other respected members of the congregation.

## OTHER ISSUES

### ACCOMMODATION

This is often one of the most important matters to be resolved in the process of appointment, and, in areas where housing costs are high, some imaginative and flexible solution may be called for.

If the church is in the happy position of having a property in its ownership, or one of the members can make one available for rent or purchase, then matters may proceed swiftly. In other situations, it may be necessary for some part in the equity of the property to be held by the church, or a member, or for a loan to be made available at a reduced rate of interest, or even interest free. These arrangements will have tax and NIC implications which should be carefully weighed in advance.

Another word of warning. Circumstances can change rapidly, both in personal and family lives and in the housing market (witness the sharp price reductions in many areas between 1988 and 1990). Thus, an arrangement entered into in all good faith one year, where the nightmare scenario, if contemplated at all, is ignored for all practical purposes, can be difficult to unravel a short time later when, for example, the FSW feels it time to move on.

Again, where a rental arrangement is entered into, a particular relationship is created between landlord and tenant, and the law which governs these matters is voluminous and complex. In particular, there can be restrictions upon the ability to regain possession of a dwelling-house, as a result of statutory rights which accrue to a tenant. A clear legal agreement is vital, and precise rules for notice, etc, must be observed.

Help with the purchase of a home for occupation by a FSW is available via Stewardship Services, formerly UKET, (PO Box 99, Loughton, Essex IG10 3QI) by means of loans at a reduced rate of interest. These are available only to the church, not directly to the FSW. Further details can be obtained on application.

## CAR

The FSW will almost certainly require the use of a car to carry out his or her duties. It may be that the church is in a position to make available a vehicle or the finance to acquire one. In that case, there are tax and NIC implications for the FSW (if an employee) under the benefits legislation where the private use of a vehicle is permitted. The employing church cannot, of course, make use of the corresponding allowances which would be available if the provider were carrying on a trade.

It may be better for the FSW to provide the car, with or without help, and to claim the appropriate proportion of capital allowances and expenses relating to business use. Employers can agree with the IR to operate a 'Fixed Profit Car Scheme' (FPCS) which involves the payment of mileage allowance at a rate which gives rise to no taxable benefit if the employer reimburses 'business' mileage undertaken in the employee's private car.

Note, however, that if the employer pays an allowance which is higher than the figure worked out from this scheme, the excess is taxable. Similarly, if the employer pays less than the FPCS rates, a deduction equal to the difference can be claimed. Booklets IR132 (Employers) and 133 (Employees) give guidance and further detail.

## PENSION ARRANGEMENTS

There is currently much debate about the increasing cost of funding state pensions for an ageing population well into the twenty-first century, and general agreement that provision out of the public purse will gradually form a smaller and smaller proportion of income in retirement. It may therefore be increasingly important to make healthy provision for the FSW's retirement by ensuring that contributions towards a private pension are made.

Most churches will probably feel the administrative burdens of setting up and running an approved scheme are out of proportion to the benefit to be conferred upon one or two individuals. But the exemptions from tax for employee contributions and for income arising within the scheme are considerable, and should not be neglected.

More commonly, however, the church will need to ensure that the level of remuneration paid to the FSW is sufficient to allow him or her to commence, or continue, personal pension planning at an adequate level. Both Evangelical Alliance and Stewardship Services (formerly UKET) operate pension schemes, and may be aproached for details. Employed FSWs may make contributions which attract tax relief as Personal Pension Premiums (PPPs), at a maximum of 17.5% of net relevant earnings up to age 35, and thereafter on a rising scale up to 40% of earnings at age 61 or over (somewhat unlikely to be achieved in practice?). These figures for PPP include contributions by employers. Self-employed FSWs may pay retirement annuity premiums. Here, the allowable percentage of net relevant earnings is 17.5% up to age 50, rising to 27.5% at age 61 or over. By contrast, employee contributions, including Additional Voluntary Contributions (AVCs) by members of employers' exempt approved schemes, are restricted to 15% of remuneration for the tax year, with no carry forward or carry back provisions.

Even this short (and inadequate) summary will indicate how complex pension planning can become. Again, one can hardly stress enough that independent advice must be taken.

## CHURCH GIVING

Any church considering the engagement of a FSW should, first of all, have established a cheerful commitment to regular and systematic giving by its members. Thankfully, tax legislation has for some time joined the state in cooperation with church members to maximise the effect of their generosity. The church treasurer should persistently press these advantages, and thrust into members' hands forms pre-prepared for just this purpose. Two schemes merit particular mention (see IR66 for 'Individual Giving to Charity' and IR113 for 'Gift Aid').

### DEEDS OF COVENANT

Payments under a deed of covenant capable of lasting for at least four years will generate tax repayments to the church of an extra

30%—i.e., for every £100 pledged and paid, the church receives a total of £129.87. These figures apply for 1997–98: figures vary according to the basic rate of tax, currently 23%, and, as this has fallen, the benefits of deeds of covenant have diminished.

A word to church treasurers. A number of cases have come to our attention recently, where sloppy administration of the covenants scheme has prompted embarassing IR investigation. One must never attempt to 'cut corners', or skimp on the required documentation in this area.

GIFT AID

For the last few years, individuals have been able to take advantage also of 'Gift Aid' donations to maximise the benefit to the church. These are single cash gifts of at least £250 (net of basic rate tax), and need not be recurrent. They will clearly be of particular interest to someone whose annual income is fluctuating, or whose tenure is insecure and who would thus be reluctant to enter into a binding continuing commitment.

With both types of gift, although the charity (church) reclaims tax only at the basic rate, a donor who pays tax at the higher rate, presently 40%,is granted relief at this higher rate on the gross equivalent of the gift.

The question of church giving is so critical that a church ought not to offer an appointment to any FSW before the elders have provided comprehensive and challenging teaching on the financial responsibilities of all members. Well in advance of the FSW's arrival, they must clearly communicate to the church what the total commitment will be—i.e., not just the appropriate salary or fee, but all additional expenses (car, telephone, training, books, accommodation, NICs and pension contributions).

CONCLUDING COMMENTS

The appointment of a FSW, especially for the first time, naturally gives rise to heightened expectations and increased optimism. Church leaders and members alike need to give the new FSW the maximum encouragement and support so that the church receives the maximum benefit from the new situation.

All concerned should be aware, however, of the danger of unrealistic expectations, and should realise that changes are likely to be made which, inevitably, some will not like or approve.

It has been said, somewhat cynically but not, perhaps, unrealistically that a church can treat a new FSW in the following way:

In the first year they idolise him
In the second year they criticise him
In the third year they pulverise him.

What needs to be borne in mind is that it may well take two years before the benefits of the work and influence of a FSW can properly be seen.

If the appointment is going to work satisfactorily, it is essential that there should be a substantial measure of mutual trust, honesty and openness between the FSW and the church leadership. Any matters giving cause for concern to either party need to be raised, discussed and resolved promptly.

Should it become clear, however, after a reasonable time has elapsed, that the appointment is not right and is clearly not working well, it is important that this fact should be faced. It is far better that the appointment should be brought to an end in a sympathetic and generous manner, rather than soldiering on to the end of the pre-set contract period, bringing little but pain to all concerned.

The appointment of a FSW has, in the majority of cases, turned out to be of great benefit to the church. It is a very demanding exercise for the church leaders, but one well worth the effort. It really indicates that the church is not content with maintenance, but has the vision and the faith in God to move into mission.

# 3

# Working Relationships

John P Redfern
*Elder at West Street Chapel, Carshalton.*

*'Make every effort to keep the unity of the Spirit in the bond of peace.'*
*(Eph 4:3 )*

The Bible is always practical. In this verse, Paul reminds us that unity is important, and that a lot of effort is required if it is to be preserved. If the relationship between the FSW and the church members is going to be a good and fruitful one, then it is important to get the foundation right. This requires a great deal of effort, both in the beginning and subsequently, to maintain the good start. It is also vitally important to recognise that having a FSW in the church, possibly where you have not had one before, is first and foremost a partnership, since other leaders have a continuing role to play; they are not about to abrogate their responsibilities.

A church should also be aware that there are two traps into which the church can fall. The first is to expect your FSW to take over everything and to run every activity—after all, he or she is being paid, aren't they? Second, the coming of a FSW can radically affect the dynamics within both the leadership and the church. It is wise to recognise this at the very outset.

The purpose of appointing a FSW to a church can obviously vary. They may come to have a leadership role and to undertake the bulk of the ministry and pastoral work, or in a larger church the role may be more specialised. Alternatively, they may be involved in the youth work or the social work of the church. The remarks made below are, in the main, general in character, but in some instances they apply chiefly to those involved in a leadership and ministry role. (See chapter 8, below, for a discussion of FSWs with specialised roles.)

The patterns established need to be adapted in line with the FSW's age and maturity. A younger person coming into a position will have needs different from those of a more mature Christian. Therefore, the key elements might need modification, depending on the particular circumstances of the church.

What is written here represents the viewpoint of an elder of the church, rather than that of a FSW, although there has been some input into what has been written from the recent FSW at West Street Chapel.

## THE BEGINNING

Assuming that a good understanding has been established between the leadership of the church and the incoming worker during the selection process, then the early weeks of the appointment should be carefully monitored to ensure that:

- the job description is a true statement of the actual job;
- the terms of employment and the financial arrangements are both clearly understood and properly followed;
- ' support mechanisms' are properly in place;
- the position of the FSW in leadership, as agreed during the initial discussions, is implemented;
- there is clear understanding on both sides concerning matters of doctrine and practice, and any differences are immediately addressed.

The leadership should neither entertain unduly high expectations of what the FSW can achieve, nor should they 'leave everything to the FSW'. The FSW should take time to appreciate the dynamics of the church he or she is coming to, before pressing for change. Problems emerging at this stage should be dealt with as soon as possible, in order to reduce the possibility of them festering later.

## THE CONTINUATION

In order for the most harmonious and effective working together to occur, a number of key steps need to be stressed. This may be seen as a counsel of perfection, and, please, don't imagine that we always got it right at West Street. We didn't. However, after nine years we have learned a few things, and what follows is drawn from our collective wisdom. I hope it will be of some value, both for those embarking on using a FSW for the first time and for any who have had an unsatisfactory experience and are cautious about moving forward in this direction again.

## START AS YOU MEAN TO GO ON

I am assuming that you have conducted the selection process in the way indicated in the previous chapter. Because of its importance I will summarise it here in the light of our experience. You will have heard the applicant preach and he will have visited several times and held in-depth discussions with the elders or leadership, as well as meeting with the opinion-formers within the fellowship. Doctrine and practice will have been carefully looked at together; the vision for the task and the church will have been shared, and there are no disagreements that cannot be overcome. References will have been taken up and opinions sought from those close to the prospective FSW. If the FSW has a family then it is clear that they, too, are happy with the arrangements, for an unhappy spouse can lead to tensions and pressures which can be very difficult to overcome. There is a good understanding on both sides. The FSW is a good 'fit' and will not be a square peg in a round hole, and there is every indication that, under God's good hand, the FSW will be able to carry out the task that the leadership has worked out.

The practicalities will have been agreed. These include:

- A *job description* which clearly spells out all the tasks to be undertaken, along with a clear title of the position that the FSW will occupy which will enable both the church and, especially, the outside community to identify something about the person's role.
- A *contract* which will clearly specify the following:

*Remuneration package*, including pension arrangements. Incidentally, but importantly, do ensure that the amount to be paid is actually paid on the due date, so that the FSW need have no concern that he or she is in danger of becoming overdrawn on account of a delayed payment.

*Terms and conditions.* These will include length of the appointment (since situations change, 3 or 5 years is a good period); arrangements to review the situation and decide whether or not to extend the appointment (adequate notice of this review needs to be built into the contract to allow sufficient time for the FSW to find an alternative position should the decision be made not to renew the contract); arrangements for regular appraisal of the work done by the FSW (built in at this stage means that, when the time comes for the appraisal to be carried out, the FSW is prepared and doesn't find it sprung on him). Other matters to be decided include annual holidays, absences away from the church, a weekly day off, the number of outside speaking engagements permitted. And what about monies earned from outside engagements, and provision for attendance at conferences, retreats and the like? As much as possible needs to be anticipated and thought through in advance, in order to avoid problems or misunderstandings later on into the contract.

*Accommodation* In addition to the provision of housing there needs to be a clear understanding as to who pays what in respect of matters like: council tax, bills, telephone, hospitality.

*Position in the leadership structure* This needs to be set down clearly. Is the FSW to be an elder, or a deacon? If neither, what are the lines of communication, to whom does the FSW report, how often, and in what way? How are problems to be handled?

*Outside support team* It is most important that the FSW has people, not necessarily able to meet together, who are prepared to pray for and support the FSW. From experience in other Christian spheres I have learned that this is a vital aid to maintaining the spiritual health and vigour of the FSW. Our FSW at West Street had one person in particular with whom he empathised, with whom he met from time to time for long walks or whatever, and with whom he could share his concerns and spend time in discussion and prayer.

I make no apology for emphasising the importance of getting this first key step right. It is important to be businesslike in these matters, and it helps to establish the partnership on the right footing from the beginning. Setting things down in writing so that, if necessary, reference can be made back to them avoids confusion at a later date. A good foundation makes for a stable and profitable relationship throughout the years that the FSW is working in the church.

Having established the foundation it is important—to change the metaphor—that the goal posts should not be moved unilaterally. If, at any stage, changes are to be made, then they must be mutually explored and agreed. There is nothing more upsetting that to find that things are not what one thought they were, and that different things are now wanted of the FSW.

## COMMUNICATION

Once the relationship has been established on the right footing, then this next key element is vital and cannot be neglected at any time. In fact, it could be said to underlie all the other key elements that follow because, to a greater or lesser extent, they all come down to communication. There is need for constant and regular communication between FSW and leadership, and between the leaders and the church. It is especially helpful if a good understanding develops between the chairman, say, of the leadership and the FSW and they meet together regularly to look at the work together and to discuss forthcoming matters. Silence breeds suspicion.

It helps to have regular meetings set up so that matters can be raised without any undue feeling of something 'special' or 'ominous' about a meeting called to deal with a particular issue. They can come up in the course of the normal weekly, monthly, or whatever periodicity of meeting is set up. All this helps to nurture a good relationship

It is important that the communication is two-way, and that adequate provision is made for the FSW to communicate clearly to the leadership as well as vice versa. Thus the FSW can be given a spot at leadership meetings and at church meetings, to enable him or her to raise any matter of concern.

Such communication must be real, and not superficial. Any new idea should not be brushed aside but given careful consideration, as should any gripes. It can be helpful to air something in a preliminary way at a first meeting, and for it to be discussed more fully at the next meeting. In this way, it can simmer for a week or so and, as a result, second thoughts may emerge, after mature consideration, which are more objective. For a new idea floated in a meeting immediately puts some people on to the defensive, whereas considering it at a later meeting helps to give a better perspective on the idea. As a result, if it has merit, it has a greater chance of being accepted, perhaps with modifications, rather than being thrown out.

It is good to review the situation of the church and of the FSW from time to time, though not too often, for if you dig up a plant frequently to see if it is growing you will eventually kill it off. If the FSW is on a fixed term contract, then the discussion at the agreed date for consideration of renewal provides a great opportunity to adjust any arrangements that have been made, in the light of experience and the way in which matters are progressing in the church. It is also likely that, after a period in the position, both FSW and elders will have a clearer focus on the task that needs to be done.

A further consideration is that the nature of the work may need some adjustment in the light of the progress made by the church. For example, a number may have become new Christians, the number of almost-Christians may have grown, the age balance may have changed through additions to the church or loss of people moving to another part of the country, or by death, perhaps including some key personnel. We all know that nothing remains static for very long these days, and it is important to allow for this in the planning and in the job description.

For example, in our own church over the past nine years there has been numerical growth and the age balance has changed to a much lower age grouping, with more families being involved and a number of new Christians being nurtured. Therefore our FSW changed emphasis to a ministry that stressed teaching, prayer and pastoral care more than when he first came. His initial task had been essentially to restore stability in the church after a difficult period which had seen a number of folk leave to set up another fellowship. During the first year of his first three-year contract, he had accepted no speaking engagements outside the church, though after that initial year he had had one Sunday off each month. This modification was good for the church in two ways. It meant that others in the church were in no way excluded from taking their place in ministry; and it enabled the FSW to visit other churches where he was both refreshed and exposed to new ideas.

The leadership needs to be alert and to stand back and make an honest appraisal of the situation. For this reason we instituted a Leadershp Awayday each year, at which we had a less structured agenda and were freer to spend more time considering deeper issues than was possible at our normal monthly business meeting. We were also able to spend time in an unhurried way in worship and prayer, and to allow God to refresh us.

## DON'T LET PROBLEMS FESTER

At some stage during the contract period, tensions may well arise. These may centre on straightforward issues, such as time off in lieu, balancing outside commitments and speaking engagements, attendance at conferences, or seminars, taking of holidays etc. Or they may arise from more complex issues such as a developing personality clash, a shift in emphasis in worship, the exercise of spiritual gifts, the pace of change, undue attention being paid to one aspect of church life or even to one particular person (maybe of the opposite sex), tensions with and within the leadership etc. Sometimes the problems can be very complex where, for example, the leadership is in some way using the FSW over a conflict on, say, the pace of change or the style of worship. In such cases, the 'go-aheads' should not draw the FSW on to their side against those who want to proceed more cautiously, or vice versa. Such issues need to be debated openly and fully, prayed through, accepted by all, and then acted on.

Some of us leaders, I venture to suggest, are not very good at dealing with problems. We like to close our eyes to them, hoping that they will go away. We like to avoid confrontation and therefore back off from facing up to situations. But the problems will not go away! In fact, leaving them alone normally allows them to escalate, making it even harder to deal with them. For, with the passage of time, entrenched positions are taken and the problem may become almost impossible to resolve without a lot of hurt on both sides. If it had been tackled earlier, before people had taken up fixed positions, then nobody would have lost face and the matter could have been settled relatively happily and quickly.

It may be that the FSW is increasingly at odds with the leadership on some issues: for example, the pace of change, the style of worship, the gifts of the Spirit and their development and place within the church. Issues of this nature must be thrashed out openly and fully, with all the leadership present and adequate time allowed for these important matters to be resolved. As far as possible, factions must not be allowed to develop. The resolution of these issues depends on the leadership, as well as the FSW, agreeing to the doctrine of 'collective' leadership and abiding by the collective decision, even if it is not unanimous. Nobody should be allowed to get away with undermining a decision of this importance and nature. It may be that, after the most careful and prolonged discussion and prayer, there may be an agreement to disagree. The outcome may then have to be that the FSW should depart. In this case, as far as it is possible, the parting should be agreed to with graciousness and sensitivity.

It may be that the FSW is at odds with the leadership but at one with most of the church. This is a deep problem if the leadership is out of touch with the mood and thoughts of the church. One way forward is to hold a church meeting or meetings, perhaps with a strong neutral person from outside who commands the respect of the leadership and the church to chair and act as moderator. Where the matter goes from there depends on the outcome of the meeting(s).

A further consideration relates to the method by which the leadership comes to hold that position. Is the leadership a self-perpetuating body? Is it elected by the church members in a democratic vote? Or does the existing leadership act on advice received from the church (i.e., taking account of what people say, but making the final decision themselves)? Each leadership pattern demands a different approach, and so there is no general rule that can apply to all cases.

It may well be that the differences become too great to bridge, and therefore, the only solution is to call a halt and to negotiate a clean break, releasing the FSW from his or her contract. Even under these circumstances, it is essential to do all things decently and in order. Therefore, negotiations for the parting should be conducted amicably and thoroughly, so that neither party feels aggrieved.

## DON'T CRITICISE BEHIND THE FSW'S BACK

One of the things that can profoundly affect the morale of the FSW is discussion and criticism going on behind his or her back. The leadership should actively discourage people moaning to the leadership and not to the FSW. However, we should be very sensitive to the nature of the people making the criticisms, and whether it is destructive or constructive. If it is destructive, then the leadership should take every means to protect the FSW so that he or she does not become discouraged. As Christians, we are very good at moaning to others rather than to the person concerned. We are also very good at complaining when there is no good reason.

Nobody does things in precisely the same way as the next person, and when a FSW comes to work in a church some changes are bound to be introduced which are not to everybody's liking and may create tensions. Perhaps this means that teaching needs to be given at the appropriate time about 'the doctrine of change'. It is never feasible to encapsulate things as they are. Again, if after a certain time, one FSW is followed by another, the church must be made aware that the second person will not be a clone of the first. Inevitably, comparisons will be made, and it is important that people should be warned about the dangers that can result. For this reason, the eldership may regard the possibility of an 'interregnum' as not being in any way negative but rather constituting a bridge between one FSW and the next, reducing the risk of unfortunate comparisons being made.

## AVOID FACTIONS

One of the problems within the Corinthian church was factions. (I follow Apollos; I follow Cephas; I follow Paul.) Paul condemns this most strongly. In the same way it is important for today's church to avoid falling into the same trap of developing factions or cliques within the church, centring on the FSW. It is easy for the FSW to gravitate towards those to whom he or she relates most easily. We, as the leadership, must endeavour to discourage this and help the FSW to spread their friendship evenly, as far as this is possible. Again, help may be found in the outside support person who can be alerted to helping the FSW to avoid factions forming.

## LOOK FOR THE TELL-TALE SYMPTOMS

For whatever reason, there are occasions when a FSW feels down, tired, or stale. There has been some reason for discouragement and the sparkle has gone. How can this be tackled? Three ways may be suggested.

One is to ensure that the FSW has someone outside the church, or at the very least outside the leadership, to whom the FSW can relate easily; to whom they can pour out their troubles without any fear of criticism or judgment being made; with whom they can go for a long walk or play a round of golf; with whom they can pray in depth. Of course, this needs to be in place before the down period, so that a bond of trust already exists, enabling the FSW to go for support with a real feeling of confidence, knowing that he or she will get a sensitive and proper hearing.

Second, the leadership ought to be sufficiently sensitive to the situation to act appropriately by arranging, for example, for the FSW to go away for a few days, on retreat or whatever. This may include providing the wherewithal, for the problem may even be a financial one!

Third, it may be that the FSW needs to undertake some form of training so that he or she can undertake a task more effectively. The leadership needs to recognise this and to identify the type of training to be undertaken. It may be practical, such as learning computer skills or time management, or learning listening skills, or taking a general or bereavement counselling course.

## CONCLUSIONS

The above may sound like a counsel of perfection, but attention to these key elements will handsomely repay the leadership of a church. To sum up, they are: good relationships; good communication; openness and tolerance; trust and understanding; alongside the avoidance of favouritism.

Always remember that the position of both FSW and spouse can be a very lonely one, and the leadership should endeavour to show friendship and consideration by giving hospitality, as well as introducing that little (or not so little) surprise from time to time. As already mentioned, we at West Street Chapel have fallen down on some of the key elements from time to time, but we have learned from experience that they are all important and conducive to a good working relationship within the church.

# 4

# Roles and Priorities

Graham Poland

*Pastor of Grosvenor Church, Barnstaple.*

It is only fair to say that much of what follows is seen from the perspective of a 'financially-supported worker'.[11] If a church member or elder had been asked to comment on this subject, different issues might well have been raised. I propose to confine myself to key issues, as seen from the worker's point of view.

## WHAT'S IN A NAME?

The name or title given to a person working full-time in a church **is** important. To the church it conveys what the elders perceive the person's role to be; to the outside community it identifies a point of contact; more importantly, to the worker it conveys what is expected of him or her.

I remember some years ago having an interview with the elders of a church, with a view to coming and working with them. 'What would you see me doing, if I came?', I innocently asked, wondering where they set the priority. One of the elders gave the ambiguous reply: 'Well, we would just appreciate you moving in and out amongst us.' Visions of this ghost-like figure floating through the church came to my mind. I should have heard the warning bell in his reply. They were not clear in their own minds as to what they wanted, and I later discovered that their concept of full-time leadership was somewhat different to mine.

It seems that they wanted someone from a younger generation who would head up their youth work, but who would also be available through the day to do the pastoral visiting they had neglected. Each of them may well have had their own concept of what the FSW would do, but evidently they had not discussed it with each other. A lot of subsequent misunderstandings could have

---

[11] For the most part I am using this revision of the term 'full-time worker'.

been avoided if only they had taken time to consider their need, and had clearly defined it. I, also, was at fault for not picking up the signs at the interview stage.

A name can help to define the role. Some names specify a particular function, rather than a position; for instance, 'community worker' or 'youth worker', where the remit is to work specifically amongst a group of people rather than assume a church leadership responsibility. Some names betray what you do *not* want them to be doing; for instance, 'pastoral worker' may well be saying: 'We want someone who will visit, but we do not want a pastor' (a valid enough role, so long as everyone is clear about it). Other terms I have heard include 'evangelist', 'pastoral evangelist', 'Bible teacher' and 'full-time elder'.

The choice of a name goes deeper. It can, in fact, betray the position of the church vis a vis 'Brethrenism'. The title 'full-time worker' has a unique connotation, anchored in the peculiarities of the 'Brethren' movement. Originally, it referred to an itinerant evangelist or Bible teacher (a 'home' worker, as opposed to an overseas missionary). It then evolved with changing circumstances into an umbrella term to describe a person with a settled ministry in one or more churches. As 'Brethren' churches increasingly took on their own workers, they were faced with the dilemma of what to call them. The continued use of 'full-time worker' in such a setting suggests almost a subliminal deprecatory view of pastoral ministry—a reluctance to be identified as having a pastor/minister for fear of losing a 'Brethren' distinctive. What are we really afraid of, if that is the case? Is it a one-man preaching ministry, or is it a dictatorial authority figure? It may be that our understanding of a denominational pastor/minister's role is at fault; or that we are actually more traditionally 'Brethren' than we thought we were.

The irony, of course, is that 'Brethren' missionaries have had to assume the name of 'pastor' for generations, largely for legal purposes. My father has been known as a '*pastor evangélico*' ever since he started missionary work in Portugal in 1951. To those inside and outside the church it is no more than a name. It seems strange that, in the UK, we make such a fuss about it. But then, one of the perennial weaknesses of the 'Brethren' has been arguing over words and, in the process, completely missing the real issue.

## FIRST AMONG EQUALS

The real issue, surely, has to do with our philosophy of leadership. Is there such a thing as a gift of leadership, and do a group of leaders still need a leader? The 'Brethren' insistence on plurality of leadership has strengths and weaknesses. The many strengths are obvious, not least the safeguard against the corrupting potential of absolute power. One of the weaknesses, though, can be a lack of initiative. To use the analogy of a goalmouth scramble; if every defender waited for someone else to go for the ball, the opposition would soon pounce. A team captain's role is to prevent that happening. Nobody, however, is going to suggest that his role is more important than anyone else's; but in a team there needs to be a captain.

It is not imperative that the person who is 'full-time' should be a leader of the leaders. It is ideal if they can be, as they will be the ones who can invest creative time in thinking through initiatives. Maturity and experience will inevitably determine their suitability for such a role. If they are not to assume it, then someone else in eldership needs to be in that position before a worker is invited, and that needs to be pointed out to the worker. A good relationship between the two will be vital, so careful consideration as to their compatability in personality and vision is needed before an appointment is made.

A key question to be asked is whether the person is being invited to do a particular job (e.g., establish links with the community by starting playgroups and youth clubs etc), or is being given a role within the church that demands being part of the recognised leadership. I have known of many tensions created where workers have been appointed in a church but have not been recognised as elders. They have had to function in a kind of 'no man's land' between congregation and leadership, nobody knowing in which camp they were meant to be.

The more responsibility a worker is given, the more decision-making is required. Will authority be given appropriate to the responsibility? The goal of both worker and elders is to create a team where all are for one and one is for all. A strong team spirit will produce an instinctive sense of whether a decision can be made, knowing the 'mind' of the rest already, or whether consultation is needed. Working as part of a team of elders is, therefore, a healthy safeguard for a full-timer.

It also helps to prevent the loneliness and isolation so many Christian workers feel. A team of elders should provide a cushion of support around the worker, rather than be a source of frustration and tension. This, obviously, is a precious relationship forged by prayer and the work of the Spirit, and cannot be fabricated.

I listened to two FSWs recently, as they spoke to me about their respective churches. One of them referred to his 'elders'; the other referred to his 'fellow-elders'. There was a world of difference in how they viewed the task facing them. The first was using all his energy to contend with the leadership; the other was shoulder-to-shoulder with his elders, serving the Lord.

Relating to other church members is often another point of tension. One of the hidden pressures faced by full-time 'workers' is that of isolation. It is a lonely world when you are the only one in the church who is considered to be a 'professional' rather than a volunteer. There may be resentment on the part of some if they are paying for you. They may see you as being indebted to them or even employed by them. If you forge deep friendships with church members you may be accused of favouritism, and it may create dilemmas regarding confidentiality. Many of the issues you want—and need—to talk about and unburden to someone generally concern the church, and you sense the inappropriateness of sharing them with church members. In some cases, particularly with new Christians, they may see you as a kind of 'boss' and either hero-worship you as some spiritual giant, or avoid you. Either way, it isolates you. Friendships outside the church can help, but, above everything else, a good relationship with the elders is vitally important.

## MANAGER, CAPTAIN OF A SHIP, OR POLITICIAN?

Recently, I enrolled in an evening class at our local college. My main purpose was to retain some contact with non-Christians. On my first night, I anticipated being asked questions like 'What is your job?', or 'What do you do?' I could think of many descriptions, though none of them fully captured the exact role I fitted into as a FSW. As it happened, nobody was very interested in what I did; but it got me thinking about some of the roles a FSW might fulfil.

A larger church may well need a manager to manage the workforce; to interact with key people, and to ensure that every department is working efficiently. James Dunn[12] differentiates between the roles of management and leadership, and concludes that both are needed for effective church leadership. If I have one regret about my training for Christian ministry, it is that I did not acquire more training in management skills—especially in the unique field of working with a volunteer workforce.

As you assess what is needed in a worker for your church, you may decide that you want someone whose role is in dealing with people. The danger in appointing someone with that in mind is that they will spend all their time dealing with paper and have no time to deal with managing people. The weight of administration in a

---

[12]  *The Effective Leader*, Kingsway, 1995, p18.

large church could kill a FSW. Elders and others need to share that responsibility or, ideally, the church may want to appoint a part- or full-time administrator.

Another role that often causes confusion when appointing a worker is best highlighted by comparing the relationship between a ship's captain and a helmsman. Peter Wagner draws attention to the Greek word used in 1 Corinthians 12:28, translated 'admini- strations'. It is a word for a helmsman. He says:

> The helmsman is the person in charge of getting a ship to its destination. That is a perfect description of the person to whom God has given the gift of administration. The helmsman stands between the owner of the ship and the crew. The owner of the ship makes the basic decisions as to what is the purpose of the voyage, where the ship is going, and what it is to do after it gets there . . .The helmsman is expected to make the decisions necessary to solve problems as they arise so that the goals are accomplished and the ship gets to where the owner wants it.[13]

Do we see the role of the 'financially-supported worker' as that of a ship's captain making decisions as to where the ship is going, or that of a helmsman doing all the work, but having no time to plot where the ship is ultimately heading? Churches with vision are always churches with a leader who is a visionary. Such a person may or may not be the one who is full-time, but usually the two go hand-in-hand.

What, however, you may really be wanting, without admitting it, is a politician—somebody who is going to sweet-talk the various factions of the church into some kind of unity. I have known of churches where the atmosphere has been like a tinderbox about to explode, and a poor, unsuspecting FSW was being brought in to try to defuse the situation!

Time teaches you that you are never going to please everybody, so leaders need to have the courage of conviction and lead from the front. A FSW will be most effective when the church has a leader- ship that knows where it is going and takes the church with them: a leadership that leads by conviction rather than by consensus. Sometimes the task of the FSW is to ensure that that happens—to galvanise the leadership so as to mobilise the church. Appointing one merely to 'keep the peace' is grossly unfair and unrealistic.

Where are you going as a church, and what kind of roles are crucial to getting there? It may well be that existing elders are best equipped to fulfil certain roles, and what you are left with is an obvious gap. That could be the role you are calling a FSW to slot into.

---

[13]    *Your spiritual gifts can help your church grow*, p156.

## JACK OF ALL TRADES, OR MASTER OF ONE?

The dilemma facing many churches is the dilemma of knowing what should take priority. So many ministries are equally valid, but may not have the same priority of importance. Unless you prioritise, you may find yourself sucked in to every ministry, with each department feeling that they have an equal claim on your services. You will end up being asked to lead the children's work, the youth club, the ladies' meeting; to preach, visit, clean the toilets, paint the church, take people to hospital, counsel, and take funerals and weddings. Often these are things which a man (or woman) has to do when working full-time with a church, especially a small church. It is not always possible to avoid spreading your time between numerous tasks and, to a certain extent, it is a frustration we all face in church work.

It is far better, however, when what a man (or woman) does comes out of an understanding of their spiritual gifts and the consequent priorities dictated by the possession of those gifts. That surely is the key to getting the best out of everybody, especially a FSW. What has God gifted them to do well? How does that correspond to our stated priority needs? Should we not, therefore, release them to do what they are gifted to do and protect them from everyone else's agenda for them? It is important that the elders state that to the church, and then periodically review the situation with the worker, in order to ensure that it happens.

Elders may also need to encourage workers to invest their time wisely according to their gifts, and help them to avoid the 'tyranny of the urgent'. Encouragement involves affirmation, and they will regularly need to know that they are valued, and that their ministry is appreciated.

On-going training in their sphere of ministry is important, so that they can sharpen their skills and become even more effective. This is particularly necessary where a worker has devoted a number of years to the church already, and is in danger of growing 'stale'. Elders, again, must ensure that encouragement is given to take this training, especially where costs are involved. And the church should budget to cover at least part of those costs.

## 'IT IS BETTER TO PUT TEN MEN TO WORK . . .'

Ultimately, the greatest sign of failure in appointing a FSW is when the worker ends up doing all the work. It was D L Moody who said: 'It is better to put ten men to work than to do the work of ten men.' All FSWs would do well to heed the wisdom of that statement.

Appointing someone full-time should result in more work being done by church members, rather than less.

The role of the FSW should be that of facilitating and training; enabling others to discover their gifts and releasing them into their ministries. An example of this would be the training of house group leaders. The burden for pastoral care can thereby be shared out, teaching the church to see the house group leaders as a first port of call. Such an approach pre-empts the development of a 'dependency' mentality where the full-timer is seen as the only person qualified to counsel or advise.

Basically, the goal of FSWs should be to multiply themselves rather than divide themselves between a hundred equally demanding tasks.

## STOCK-TAKING AND VISION-BUILDING

Your church may be at the stage of looking for a FSW, or replacing one who is about to move on. Some of the preceding issues should be assessed, with certain fundamental question being asked prayerfully. The elders may need to do some stock-taking, asking questions such as: 'Where are we as a church?'; 'Are we inviting a worker because we are growing or because we are dying?'; 'Where do our strengths and weaknesses lie?'; 'Where could we use a worker to greatest effect?'. They may need to ask hard, direct questions about the present leadership structure, and the compatibility of a FSW. Are the needs of the church likely to be served best by appointing an existing elder, or importing fresh blood?

Having assessed your present position, pray through where you feel God is calling you to be. What is your vision? Do you have a mission statement showing clearly where you are going as a church? Would a worker want to join you because they sense you are people with a vision?

Then take the time to share the vision within the church. Create a climate of hope and expectancy, building faith in what God is able to do. In my own ministry, I have observed that whenever God has brought revival in church life it has always called for a step of faith to be taken, often by those who are entrusted with leadership. When godly leaders are prepared to step out in faith and with vision, others will follow.

When God is *your* leader, the possibilities for the future are limitless.

# 5

# Maintaining the Spiritual Glow

Victor Jack
*Counties Evangelist.*

A number of events and passages in the Bible indicate that God's people can 'glow' with the glory of God as they live their lives in communion with him. After being in God's presence for forty days and forty nights, Moses came down from Mount Sinai 'not aware that his face was radiant because he had spoken with the Lord' (Exod 34:29–35). The Psalmist wrote, 'Those who look to him are radiant; their faces are never covered with shame.' (Psa 34:5) We may not be able to explain it, or even be conscious of it, but an inward transformation takes place in our hearts, while in communion with God, which is expressed in our faces. 'The face is the mirror of the soul.' Paul emphasised this truth when he wrote to the Christians in Corinth: 'We, who with unveiled faces all contemplate the Lord's glory, are being transformed into his likeness with ever-increasing glory, which comes from the Lord, who is the Spirit.' (2 Cor 3:18) If we are to maintain our spiritual glow, we will need constantly to focus our gaze on the Lord Jesus and fellowship with him. Bishop Festo Kivengere made this clear when he wrote:

> Revival means refocussing. You know that a mirror reflects the thing on which it is focussed. If your life is focussed on Jesus Christ you will reflect His glory. But if it is focussed on yourself and your own efforts, that is all you will reflect. If you are focussed on your friends you are going to reflect them and their disappointing experiences. If you are focussed on your church and its services and ministers, you are going to reflect all your complaints about the church. Whatever you are focussed on you are going to reflect. Revival means focussing your gaze on your glorious Lord.

Romans 12:11 is a key verse: 'Never be lacking in zeal, but keep your spiritual fervour serving the Lord.' J B Phillips paraphrased this: 'Let us keep the fires of the Spirit burning as we do our work for the Lord.' A good example of a man who reflected God's glory, and served him with devotion was John the Baptist, of whom it was written, 'He was a burning and shining light.' (John 5:35, AV) The question we have to answer is: 'How do we maintain our spiritual glow; how do we keep alive our enthusiasm and love for the Lord?' But before we can suggest answers, we must look at some of the pressures we face that dampen down the fire of God's Spirit in our hearts, and destroy our love and commitment to him.

## LOSING OUR SPIRITUAL GLOW

While the various pressures I shall mention apply particularly to those involved in 'full-time Christian work', they mostly apply also to any of us who seek to serve God.

### FINANCIAL PRESSURES

We all have homes to maintain, cars to run, families to keep, ministries to keep going, and offices to run. To help with the increased costs, wives often have to go out to work, which can create even more pressure. At times we can find it difficult to keep our heads above water. The materialistic spirit of the age can so eat into our hearts that we can begin to envy the prosperity of our friends and even regret getting so involved in Christian ministry. This hand to mouth existence can become a wearying business. How easy it is for us to forget that Jesus promised that, if we 'seek first His kingdom . . . all these things [the necessities of life] will be given to us as well. Therefore', he continued, 'do not worry about tomorrow for tomorrow will worry about itself. Each day has enough trouble of its own.' (Matt 6:33,34)

### SOCIAL PRESSURES

We may experience an identity crisis because, although we are called evangelists, pastors, ministers or elders, no one in society really knows what those names mean. The exposure in the media of Christian ministers guilty of serious moral sins does nothing to improve our image. Some of the questions we are asked may seem threatening—even embarrassing. 'What do you do all day?' 'Where does the money come from?' 'Have you ever wished you had a proper job?' When our children are ridiculed at school because their dad is a preacher we can feel hurt and distressed for their sake. While we are prepared to suffer in the cause of the gospel, it is much more difficult to cope if our children are persecuted because of what we do.

## INTELLECTUAL PRESSURES

The message we preach and treasure is widely ridiculed and discredited. If we accept the historicity of certain events recorded in the Bible we are regarded as intellectually naive. If we uphold chastity before marriage and fidelity after marriage we are considered to be out of date, narrow minded, puritanical etc. Today, we have added pain arising from the crisis of faith within the church. An increasing number of leading churchmen have openly and unashamedly said that they no longer hold to some of the fundamentals of our faith. They state their case so powerfully that many are convinced. The man in the street is impressed, and the man in the ministry depressed!

## MARITAL PRESSURES

Marriage is meant to be 'a duet, not a duel', yet involvement in Christian ministry can bring tension, division and resentment. We may be guilty of putting unnecessary pressure on our partners by giving the impression that we have time for everyone else; but not for them. We may fall into the trap of 'trying to win the world, but losing our own families'. There are far too many bitter and hurting partners who feel isolated and marginalised because of their husband's or wife's ministry. Overcoming this problem is not easy unless there is discussion and an agreement as to how each is to operate. A person can serve God only as far as their partner will allow them. Some parents have the added problem of seeing their children grow up to reject their faith. Our children are an extension of us, so when they do well we purr with pride, but when they do badly we can react with anger and frustration. Family tensions can create enormous pressures which often cripple our spiritual progress and destroy our joy in the Lord.

## EMOTIONAL PRESSURES

When we are not at peace with God or ourselves as well as with others around us, because of unresolved conflicts, our emotions can tear us apart and destroy our sense of wellbeing. A difficult marriage, rebellious teenagers, shortage of money, personality clashes in the church, undeserved criticism of our ministry: these are some of the things that wear us down and break our hearts. Should these problems continue, month after month and even year after year, we can easily fall into a pit of self-pity and depression.

SPIRITUAL PRESSURES

There are difficulties we have to come to terms with, because of the nature of our Christian involvement, that few people appreciate. The pressure of seeing few results, even though we are working hard and serving God faithfully can be hard to bear. This lack of fruit in our ministry is often highlighted when we attend a conference and hear the wonderful success stories of others. 'What are we doing wrong?'; 'Why isn't God blessing me as he is blessing them?': these are some of the painful questions we may find ourselves asking. The burden of wanting to see God at work in our locality can become heavy indeed, especially when fervent prayer seems to go unanswered. Some are working in difficult environments—inner city areas, large housing estates, drug centres and multi-racial districts and the like. At times the problems can seem to be overwhelming. Others are working with difficult or disadvantaged people—those who are suffering from various addictions, mental illness, physical disabilities, etc. Certain people may treat us as psychological props and drain away our physical and spiritual resources. It is not easy to train them to lean more on God and less on us. When they phone for the twentieth time it is easy to give in to despair and want to catch the slow boat to Tarshish!

I stood with a discouraged friend on the beach watching wave after wave crash on the seashore during a violent storm. He turned to me and said: 'These waves piling in, one after the other, are a picture of all the pressures and problems mounting up against me. No sooner have I negotiated one, than another is looming large before me. I can handle a few, but when I look to the horizon and see so many other waves coming, I sense that, eventually, I will be overwhelmed.'

How do we go on 'maintaining the spiritual glow' when everything around seems to be conspiring to dampen down the fires of God's Spirit within us?

## MAINTAINING THE SPIRITUAL GLOW

What practical steps can we take in order to maintain our spiritual balance in a crazy world? Is there anything we can do to 'keep the fires of the Spirit burning as we do our work for the Lord' (J B Phillips on Rom 12:11)?

LEARN TO DISTANCE OURSELVES FROM OUR PROBLEMS

There is great value in physically removing ourselves from the arena of our activity, in order to be in a different environment where God can speak to us without the distraction of familiar and pressing things around us. I find it difficult to relax and focus on God in my office where there are always things crying out to be done; but a walk through the fields where I can be alone with God, without any disturbance, always leads to relaxation of the mind and refreshment of the spirit. Here are two biblical examples of men who found spiritual renewal by distancing themselves from their problems.

### Habakkuk (Hab 2:1)

His prophecy begins with a sigh from the heart because of the unanswered questions in his mind over the problems in his world. It ends with a man who has a song in his spirit because of the way he responded to the pressures that had threatened to overwhelm him. Having groaned under the weight of all his complaints against God, he then made a strategic decision: 'I will stand at my watch and station myself on the ramparts; I will look to see what he will say to me.' He climbed up to the watchtower on the city walls in order to get away from the turmoil of life and to put himself in a position where he would stop complaining against God and allow God to speak to him. Habakkuk's outlook and ministry were transformed as a result. We, too, need to find a way of detaching ourselves from the things that perplex us and threaten to cripple us spiritually.

### Asaph (Psa 73:16,17)

Asaph was a man in a position similar to that of Habakkuk. Deeply troubled about the way in which the wicked prospered and the righteous suffered, unresolved conflict developed in his life with the result that his heart was grieved, his spirit became embittered and his feet almost slipped from the pathway of faith. 'When I tried to understand all this', he later confessed, 'it was oppressive to me'. Feeling under pressure and deeply burdened in spirit he made a decision, like that of Habakkuk, to step back from the problems and to give God the space to speak to him. So, he later added, his problems persisted only 'till I entered the sanctuary of God: then I understood'. God gave him a new perspective on life which transformed his outlook.

### MATCH INCREASING ACTIVITY WITH INCREASING PRAYER

The perfect example of this principle is seen in the life of the Lord Jesus. 'Crowds of people came to hear him and to be healed of their sicknesses. But Jesus often withdrew to lonely places and prayed.' (Luke 5:15,16) The demands and pressures that surrounded his life, day after day, stand out on every page. The draining effect on his personality of teaching the crowds, healing the sick and travelling over rough terrain, often in intense heat, as well as facing the hostility of the Jewish leaders and the lack of faith in his disciples, must have left him physically whacked and emotionally exhausted. Once he was so tired that he fell asleep in a small boat during a violent storm. How did Jesus handle all this pressure and 'maintain the spiritual glow'? The answer is that he 'often withdrew to lonely places and prayed'. And he encouraged his disciples to do the same. Once, when 'so many people were coming and going that they did not even have a chance to eat, he said to them, "Come with me by yourselves to a quiet place and get some rest." ' (Mark 6:31) Jesus found that the best answer to a busy life was to withdraw from it and spend time in communion with his father in order to receive fresh strength and to renew his spiritual perspective. We need to 'beware of the barrenness of a busy life'.

In one of his poems, T S Eliot speaks of 'the silence that can be heard between the waves of the sea'. What a vivid picture of the stillness and healing we can find in the presence of God in the midst of the relentless moving in upon us of the pressures of life. 'Be still and know that I am God' (Psa 46:10) is something we all know but rarely experience in the rat race of life. Pascal once said: 'One of the ways in which man brings most trouble upon himself is by his inability to be still.' How slow we are to learn this lesson. It was given fresh meaning in a home at Bethany where Martha was 'distracted by all the preparations that had to be made', while Mary 'sat at the Lord's feet listening to what he said' (Luke 10:39,40). In the midst of all Martha's fretting and fuming, Jesus issued a gentle but firm rebuke: 'Martha, Martha, you are worried and upset about many things, but only one thing is needful. Mary has chosen what is better, and it will not be taken from her.' How prone we are to become worried and upset about 'many things', and to forget that only 'one thing' is needed—to take time out to be with our Lord, to enjoy his presence and to let him speak to us.

How appropriate for all of us who carry heavy workloads and face constant pressure are the words of Longfellow: 'Let us labour for an inward stillness and an inward healing, that perfect silence where the lips and heart are still, and we no longer entertain our own imperfect thoughts and vain opinions, but God himself speaks in us and we wait, and seek to do his will and do that only.'

We need, with a need beyond anything words can express, to step out of the busy whirlpool of our activities, in which we so often lose our sense of balance and perspective, and to stand alone with God. Only then can we imbibe something of the stillness of eternity and be renewed in mind and spirit for the next stage of the battle.

## TAKE TIME OUT FOR LEISURE AND RELAXATION

How easy it is to become a workaholic in Christian service because there is so much to be done and so few to do it. We can become like the man of whom it was written: 'He threw his life away in a vain attempt to be everywhere, to do everything and to act for everyone.' We must beware of allowing an atmosphere of rush to invade the whole of life so that we create havoc of our nervous systems. We need to take time on a regular basis in order to relax. Recreation is to the mind what sleep is to the body; we must not neglect either. All of us need regular patterns of sleep, and some need more sleep than others. Le Maitre wrote: 'I must go to bed early because I have a great many things to do.' Not many of us function well when we are tired, yet we often give the impression that we are tired at the very time when we need to be keen and alert.

A lovely story told about John the Evangelist illustrates the need for relaxation and leisure. One day he was discovered by a huntsman, out in the country amusing himself with a tame partridge on his hand. The huntsman asked how such a holy man could spend his time in so unprofitable an occupation. John replied: 'Why do you not always carry your bow bent?' The huntsman responded: 'If it were always bent, I feel it would lose its spring and become useless.' John used this illustration to justify his use of time in order to relax: 'Be not surprised, then, that I should remit a little of my close attention of spirit to enjoy a little recreation, that I may afterwards employ myself more fervently in divine contemplation.'

To lay down a responsibility for a while is to return to it refreshed, and to complete it more quickly. Our minds and bodies need rest and change. It is important to keep our bodies fit and our minds alert. If we do so, we will find that we will cope better with the problems and crises of life, and maintain our spiritual fervour with less difficulty.

## SHARE WITH FRIENDS WHO WILL SHARPEN YOUR SPIRITUAL RESOLVE

We were never meant to go it alone and operate like lone rangers who have broken away from the pack. We need the support and mutual encouragement of our fellow Christians. How good it is to have a friend with whom we can share our burdens with confidence, and how enriching to spend time together in prayer. We can do so much to inspire and motivate one another. The Bible teaches us to 'carry each other's burdens' (Gal 6:2) and to 'consider how we may spur one another on towards love and good deeds . . . and to encourage one another' (Heb 10:24,25). It can be such a stimulating experience to have a friend with whom we can share God's word and enjoy the presence of Jesus in prayer. 'As iron sharpens iron, so one man sharpens another.' (Prov 27:17) Most of us need massive doses of encouragement in our service for God. How often God has used the words of another Christian to keep us on our feet spiritually. What a blessing Jonathan was to David.

Those of us involved as Christian ministers can find great blessing and refreshment by meeting with other ministers in our town and district. We all serve the same master, and face the same problems, so we ought to be the ones who strengthen each other's hands in the work of God. In our home town of Bury St Edmunds I have the joy and privilege of meeting each Friday morning with a group of leaders for an hour's prayer together. These are times of heaven on earth when twelve to fourteen leaders meet, not to discuss church politics, but to pour out our hearts in praise and prayer. I always leave feeling renewed and refreshed, ready to throw myself into the day's work.

SEEK THE CREATIVITY OF THE HOLY SPIRIT IN OUR DEVOTIONAL LIFE

It is so easy to drop into a rut and become hidebound to a certain style of 'Quiet Time'. We need to ask God to help us find ways and means that are appropriate for us to ensure that our times of Bible reading are meaningful, and our prayer life uplifting. We are promised that 'those who wait on the Lord will renew their strength. They will soar on wings like eagles; they will run and not grow weary, they will walk and not faint.' (Isa 40:31) God can minister to us in this way as we commune with him through prayer and reading scripture.

Books and tapes on this subject can give us helpful ideas which may put fresh life and meaning into our times with God. Many have found worship and teaching tapes to be a great blessing while travelling to work. Others discover that it is easier to pray while walking rather than sitting, or to pray and sing aloud rather than in silence. Some find it a great help to keep a prayer diary and to record answers as an encouragement to further prayer. Others write prayers as a response to the scriptures they have been reading. Many and varied are the means we can use to maintain our devotional life with the Lord, which then becomes the source of our strength in our ministry.

## BE CONSTANTLY FILLED WITH THE HOLY SPIRIT

There will often be times when we feel empty and discouraged as
well as dry and barren in spirit. At such times we need to remember
the words of Simon Peter: 'Lord to whom shall we go? You have
the words of eternal life.' (John 6:68)

How grateful I am to an older Christian who encouraged me to
fall on my knees when feeling inadequate and unworthy, and to ask
the Holy Spirit to come and fill this empty vessel afresh. How
beautifully simple, and yet how powerful, are the words of Jesus to
those of us who feel from time to time that we have 'blown it' and
have lost our way: 'If any man is thirsty, let him come to me and
drink. Whoever believes in me, as the Scripture has said, streams
of living water will flow from within him. By this he meant the
Spirit, whom those who believed on him were later to receive.'
(John 7:37–39)

Our spiritual condition is summed up in the word 'thirst'. This
is a word which we don't readily understand in our culture since
we are part of the twenty per cent who have water piped into our
homes. In the Middle East during the time of Jesus, water was a
precious commodity. To run out of water, when on a journey in
the intense heat of summer, would lead to dehydration and death,
unless a fresh supply could be found. A traveller would become
desperate for water, just as we long with all our hearts for renewal
and refreshment in the Holy Spirit when we are out of touch with
God. This was the yearning of the Psalmist when he surfaced the
deep longings of his heart: 'O God you are my God, earnestly I seek
you; my soul thirsts for you, . . . in a dry and thirsty land where
there is no water.' (Psa 63:1) The same *cri de coeur* is found in Psalm
143:6: 'I spread out my hands to you; my soul thirsts for you like
a parched land.'

The cure for our spiritual dryness when we know we have lost
our 'spiritual glow' is to come once more to the Lord Jesus, the
fountain of living water, and ask him to fill us afresh with his Holy
Spirit. He will keep his promise, filling us with himself, and flowing
from us like a refreshing stream bringing blessing to others.

# 6

# Family Pressures

Jean Campbell
*Counties Evangelist.*

We live in a world where pressures abound, and many people suffer from stress. In previous generations the workload was equally hard—probably harder—but many of the present day tensions were hardly known.

As the pace of life gets faster, we are inundated with all sorts of information about this and that. We are faced with many choices. There was a time when life was comparatively straightforward, but now we have to decide between so many alternatives!

There is also the pressure to succeed. This may come from the family, with parents putting undue pressure on their children to do well; from schools which are anxious to keep as near as possible to the top of the exam results table; or from employers.

It seems strange that the pressures on Christians are sometimes greater than those experienced by non-Christians. Yes, we know that there is a heavenly father who cares for us, and who urges us to 'cast our burdens' upon him; but most of us know that this is often easier said than done. There are so many verses in the Bible which urge us to work harder, not to spare ourselves, to press ahead more earnestly towards the goal set before us. The more committed we are, the more pressure we seem to put upon ourselves!

Christians in full-time service have their own peculiar pressures. There are many reasons for this. We may be striving to conform to the stereotype of a 'busy Christian worker', or trying to live up to the expectations of others. The fact that we are attempting to serve people in desperate need, both of the gospel and of the milk of human kindness, can sometimes increase the pressure. So do the family commitments which are the particular topic of this chapter.

We may even reach the point where, although we say that we are justified by faith, we act as if we are justified by works! We may need to sit down and ask ourselves if the expectations we have of ourselves and other people are too high. Do we try too hard?

## WHO COUNTS AS FAMILY?

For most of us, the immediate family consists of husband, wife and children. In the case of those of us who are involved in full-time Christian work, the parents are partners, but, by adolescence, the children may not be quite as sympathetic to the situation as they were.

The wider family may include parents who are not supportive in the work, and who may not even be Christians. The disadvantage of this is that you are deprived of family back-up (although one solution is to adopt a granny from the church), but the advantage is that life can be lived as you feel right, without conforming to the idea of what the family think you should be doing! As the years go by, ageing parents who live miles away bring growing concern that you are not able to be near enough to help them as much as you would like.

## ROUTINE PRESSURES

The main difference between those working in 'secular' employment and full-time Christian workers seems to be the urgency of the everyday matters with which we have to deal. Whereas statistics and computer work can be programmed according to its urgency, we always seem to be dealing with people whose demands are immediate. Such people seem to think that our lives are their own private possession: 'Can you give me a lift?'; 'Can you visit . . . ?'; 'Will you pray for . . . ?'; 'Can I come in for a few minutes?' The urgency of the demands can bring considerable pressure, when added to our existing commitments. This can be coped with only by liberal doses of 'the joy of the Lord' (Neh 8:10) and the prayer, 'Give your servant success today' (Neh 1:11).

Another source of stress can be the disappointments faced: for example when a programme we have set up which seemed to be going well begins to lose its effectiveness; or when someone who has trusted the Lord seems to regress. At such times it is easy to lose heart and lack commitment.

Finances can create pressure. There is nothing like a shortage of money for your family's needs to make you feel totally materialistic! On the other hand, lack of necessary resources can strengthen faith. Wonderful stories can be told of the Lord's provision. He knows what we need even before we ask (Psa 37:25), but one of the lessons we have to learn if that, if we move out of the Lord's will, the manna will cease. We have to move when the fire/cloud moves.

Housing can cause problems. Some churches provide accommodation for full-time workers, but that still leaves the problem of later years if one is unable to buy a property. But we know that he who has led and provided all the way will continue to do so until the end.

The education and spiritual growth of our children is of prime importance. We want them to see that Christian service can be a way of life—not just something adults do. We need to be interested in what they do, spending time not only providing for their present needs but planning with them for the future, and sharing with them in whatever is of importance to them.

Another thing that can create pressure is Sunday. Often described as the Christian's busiest day of the week, it can lose its significance as a special day of rest and refreshment. Its busyness and hectic activity can sometimes make it a burden to the Christian worker with a family.

Like everyone else, the Christian worker has health pressures from time to time. These can cause distress but, on the positive side, they can teach us lessons which can be learned only in the school of experience, and which can help us empathise with the many people we meet who are going through similar experiences.

## MEANS OF OVERCOMING PRESSURES

One very important aid is prioritising. This, of course, is not always possible, but whenever it is, ration your time, ensuring that the important things are given priority.

## HUSBANDS AND WIVES

Make sure you spend quality time together. Yours is the closest relationship on earth and, like all relationships, it needs cultivating if it is to flourish—even survive. For the Christian, this is a spiritual as well as a natural bond, and we need to give each other encouragement, not only in coping with daily life, but in all aspects of Christian life and service. Make sure that your expectations of each other are not unrealistically high; share troubles as well as joys; and pray together over everything (1 Pet 5:7). Each partner needs to be able to depend on the other, even though, sometimes, they may not see eye to eye.

## PARENTS AND CHILDREN

It is essential that both partners are involved in decisions regarding the children, and that responsibility for them is shared. Children need both parents as role models.

Plan together for the future, under the hand of God. This may include moving house from one part of the country to another, involving change of schools as well as place of work. Take the needs of the children into account when making decisions, always remembering that these have to be weighed against other factors.

Whatever the cost, find time to spend together with the children, because the relationship you develop with them can set a precedent for life. Treasure them, and enjoy their company. This will give them a pattern to follow if and when they become parents. Try to instil into them a God-consciousness and a love for the Lord Jesus, by praying and reading the Bible with them. Take time to enjoy with them what they enjoy, whether it be sport, music (not always to our own taste!), or holidays. Christian camps and houseparties can be enjoyable, even though they are hard work.

But do not shrink from disciplining them (Heb 12:7–11), bearing in mind that the young ones, too, have many pressures put on them. Discipline which may sound harsh to modern ears was intended as a framework for the training and instruction which was so important a feature of home life in biblical times, and is no less important today.

In all this, be at pains to establish firmly in their minds a proper sense of self-worth. This is particularly important for the children of Christian workers who are often expected to be different from other children and to show exemplary patterns of behaviour. It is easy for them to remain under the shadow of their parents even after they have reached adolescence. As they grow older, encourage them to get involved in their own sphere of work in the church, perhaps as members of the youth or music group. Be careful that those who have not made a profession of faith do not feel rejected and become alienated.

## USE OF THE HOME

This can bring pressure as well as pleasure! Some of us regard our home as our castle, into which we retreat in order to escape the demands of the outside world. When we need this privacy, we should explain that we need to recharge our batteries, never forgetting the biblical picture of hospitality as a Christian responsibility (Heb 15:2) and a requirement for church leaders (1 Tim 3:2).

Hospitality can be demanding, often calling for normal household arrangements to be altered at short notice. This can be disruptive for us, and even more so for the children, especially if those being entertained are complete strangers (or people to whom they take an instant dislike!). Any damage caused can be limited if we keep in mind its value, and if we help the children to feel part of it by being involved, as far as this is possible, in the whole process.

Hospitality can also place a considerable burden on an already overstretched household budget. Some enlightened churches recognise this, and make provision for it. But, whether they do, or do not, our experience is that the Lord always supplies what we need.

## TIME OUT

However singleminded we are in our Christian commitment, there is a place for other interests. Our effectiveness in Christian work calls for periods of relaxation and re-creation. God has given us many good things to enjoy, so, whether our interests lie in gardening, music, first aid classes, or whatever, time should be allocated to them. We may also need to spend time acquiring skills and developing abilities. This should be seen, not as a competing demand on limited time, but as a solid investment which yields dividends.

## NON-CHRISTIAN MEMBERS OF THE FAMILY

These need our constant prayers and a double dose of love. Try to understand their problems, and encourage them to talk to you. Show the joy of the Lord, and don't go around complaining, and being a misery. Our life may not be all sweetness and light, and we have our problems; but let them see that, with Christ, there is victory.

## PREPARATION TIME

Whatever we do takes time, but the one vital thing we must not miss out on is our personal relationship with the Lord. We should constantly ask ourselves whether the 'calling' to do a particular piece of work is clearly from the Lord and, if it is, what demands it is going to make on our time.

Time for preparation is essential. Most of us have times of the day that are more suitable than others. In my case it is usually early in the morning, since I seem to be a morning person. Saturday morning, for me, is Sunday school preparation time—songs to be chosen, theme to be written, games to be tied in with the subject matter in order to reinforce the lesson. Youth work activity needs to be organised on a weekly basis, with crafts, games, cooking and epilogues. Whatever it is, time needs to be set aside for it.

## HOME AND CHURCH

In a busy life it is sometimes necessary to remind ourselves that we go to church to worship the Lord and have fellowship with others. It is not just a lifelong habit! It would be easy to be too busy to go when the preacher is someone we don't very much enjoy! Perhaps we sometimes go merely because we have a job to do: to play the organ, look after the children, or give our own children a good example. But often the Lord blesses and refreshes us when we least expect it. We belong to God, and he calls us to join with others in worshipping him, leaving jobs and family behind.

# 7

# Keeping on Top of the Job

David Clarkson
*Gospel Literature Outreach.*

Under stress? 'Phone never stops? Family struggling? Impossible deadlines? Do you know the feeling?

Full-time workers, like others in leadership, are finding themselves increasingly under pressure. The pressures are so great as to lead on occasions to a breakdown in health or in spiritual vitality.

Many strategies have been put forward to solve the problem of keeping on top of the job. The one suggested here focuses on two key issues. These are *knowledge* and *action*. We need, first of all, to gather information about ourselves and our job; and then to decide on specific courses of action.

## KNOWLEDGE

### KNOWING OURSELVES

It is important that we know our own temperament and style. For example, are we morning or evening people? Are we logical, or erratic and impulsive? A range of psychological tests exist which can help us to understand our own personality type. Among them are those by Tim La Haye on temperament and Myers Briggs on personality type. The more we discover about ourselves, the more we will be able to play to our strengths.

In the context of dealing with stress, Friedman and Roseman have been able to identify 'Type A' people who are more likely to suffer the ill effects of stress. They are very similar to Gordon MacDonald's 'driven people'. Such folk are always hurrying, cannot relax, are always planning a new project, promising themselves to slow down next week or when their current project finishes—but next week never comes and the project never finishes. If this in any way describes us, then immediate action is required.

It is also important that we should identify the spiritual gifts we have been given, and recognise that we do not possess all of them.

| AREA | PRIORITIES |
|---|---|
| FAMILY | Spend more time together<br>*Timetable one night per week for family activities* |
| LEISURE | Maintain level of fitness<br>*40 minutes walk per day*<br>Lose weight<br>*1/2 stone by September* |
| SELF | Greater discipline in prayer<br>*Timetable one hour per day*<br>Read more widely<br>*3 biographies per year, subscribe to Time magazine* |
| WORK | Improve preaching standards<br>*Computer system by August to store illustrations*<br>Complete sermon preparation by Friday, each week |
| CHURCH | Develop leadership potential<br>*Prepare leadership course by 31 December* |

Many excellent tools are available which can help us discover our gifts[14], and these can enable us to be quite clear as to the things we are good at and those at which we are not so good.

We also need to be aware of and to work on our weaknesses, but not to major on them. We must learn to focus on what we are good at. If, for example, we are good at working with children, then we should major on children's work, and let that be the main thrust of our ministry. The corollary is that we must learn to refuse to attempt to do what we are uncomfortable with, and not feel guilty about it. If, through hard and bitter experience, we have learned that we have little gift or talent in a particular area of ministry, then we must feel free to decline an invitation to be involved in that kind of service.

KNOWING OUR PRIORITIES

If we are to have any chance of keeping on top of the job, we must be clear as to our priorities. One very effective exercise is to write down at the conclusion of an evening (or day) of prayer what our priorities are for our family, leisure time, personal development, work, and church. One sentence for each heading should be enough to enable us to focus on the essentials.

---

[14] See, for example, a recent Partnership publication: Henry Ratter, *Buried Talents.*

The chart opposite illustrates the general principle. It is likely that each of these statements will be fairly general. The next stage is to be very specific as to how each priority will be achieved. Normally, this will involve identifying a specific quantity and time scale (see statements in italics).

This is a very important although, sometimes, difficult exercise, but if we are to keep on top of the job it is imperative that we be quite clear as to our own priorities, in broad outline for the year, and in specific terms for each week. The point being emphasised is that it is important for us to work to *our* agenda, and not be endlessly responding to other people's priorities.

Having arrived at a clearer understanding of our priorities, it is interesting to compare how these fit in with our ongoing commitments.

The following chart illustrates an attempt to quantify the amount of time required to undertake the range of activities to which one FSW was committed at the beginning of a sixteen-week period.

### COMMITMENTS : SEPTEMBER-DECEMBER 1995

| | | | |
|---|---|---|---|
| 1 | PREACHING | 20 sermons x 6 hrs | 120 hours |
| 2 | COURSE PREPARATION | Leadership for 90s: 20 hrs<br>Elders' Forum: 20 hrs<br>Discipleship: 40 hrs<br>Pastoral Care: 40 hrs | 120 hours |
| 3 | LECTURES | N T History: 30 hrs<br>Pentateuch: 50 hrs<br>Acts: 10 hrs | 90 hours |
| 4 | BIBLE STUDIES | | 20 hours |
| 5 | COMMITTEE MEETINGS | 30 x 4 hrs | 120 hours |
| 6 | MEETINGS (excl Sunday) | 25 x 2 hrs | 50 hours |
| 7 | PRE-MEMBERSHIP CLASSES | | 20 hours |
| 8 | PERSONAL | Prayer: 80 hrs<br>General Reading: 80 hrs<br>Recreation: 80 hrs | 240 hours |
| 9 | CHURCH VISITATION | 10hrs x 16 weeks | 160 hours |
| | | **TOTAL** | **940 hours** |
| | **TIME AVAILABLE**<br>Assume 12 hour day; 5 day week | **16 weeks** | **960 hours** |

EMERGENCIES
PLANNING/THINKING
HOME/FAMILY

An estimate was made of the amount of time required for each activity under items 1 to 9, with the total number of hours coming to 940. The assumption of a twelve-hour working day for five days a week over the sixteen-week period gave a total number of hours available as 960. This assumption did not include time for eating , mowing the lawn etc, nor did it include the time spent attending church etc on Sundays. It should also be noted that no time had yet been allowed for such aspects as emergencies, planning/thinking, or home/family.

While one may debate the various assumptions, the broad lesson to be learned is that we are often committing ourselves to more hours than we have available, and in this respect the exercise, when completed, will prove particularly valuable.

KNOWING OUR CIRCUMSTANCES

It is important to have a clear understanding of what the church expects of its FSW. Often, the expectations of the church are that the individual will be a man or woman of God who is approachable, an inspiring communicator, a worship leader, an enabler, a visionary, an evangelist, an administrator etc. We need to recognise that we can never be all of these things. We must therefore be clear as to our priorities and areas of ministry. This should be worked through with our fellow leaders, so that there is clear understanding and agreement of the main thrusts of our ministry. Where appropriate, this should be written in to an updated job description.

In this context, it is essential to have a regular meeting, as opposed to crisis meetings, with an individual or group of elders for the purpose of review and accountability (as already urged in earlier chapters). It is also important for us to be able to report back on how we have used our time, and to outline our priorities as to how we see God leading us for the future. A member of the leadership should communicate with the church, so that the members have a clear understanding of what we have been doing, and how we propose to proceed in the future.

## TAKING ACTION

MAINTAINING OUR OWN SPIRITUAL LIFE

The maintenance of spiritual integrity is absolutely vital to the life and ministry of all Christians, especially for those serving the Lord full-time. This is the subject of Victor Jack's chapter in this volume (chapter 5), so it will not be necessary to go into much detail.

Suffice it to say that we must give priority to our own personal reading; we should listen to other preachers, even if it is only on tape; and we need to apply their messages to ourselves. It is helpful to establish a prayer support group. Courses, conferences, and retreats can be very helpful. We need to receive training so that we can update ourselves, acquire new skills, or improve existing skills. We need to take time off each week.

A range of spiritual self-evaluation materials are available which could be used once or twice a year, possibly in conjunction with a prayer retreat.

MAINTAINING OUR SPIRITUAL EFFECTIVENESS

The diagram below, entitled 'Diary for September', indicates the beginnings of a weekly timetable. As we plan our week, it is important to relate back to our priorities, and timetable accordingly. This means that, if we really were serious about spending one night each week with the family, then Monday night is the only available night; so it has to be timetabled in. If we were serious about giving ten hours per week to our own devotions, then these must be timetabled in; and so on.

The hard fact is that, unless the various priorities are actually timetabled in to the diary, they will not take place.

MANAGING OUR TIME EFFECTIVELY

A number of areas are crucial in helping us to handle our time effectively.

## DIARY FOR SEPTEMBER
### (Week beginning Sunday 5 September)

|           | SUN          | MON            | TUES                              | WED             | THUR           | FRI               | SAT                           |
|-----------|--------------|----------------|-----------------------------------|-----------------|----------------|-------------------|-------------------------------|
| **Morning**   | Preaching    |                | GLO                               |                 |                |                   | Leadership Training           |
| **Afternoon** |              | High school    | 2.00 B Gilmour 4.00 Elders' Forum |                 |                |                   | Leadership Training           |
| **Evening**   |              |                | 7.00 Church Lead. Team            | Prayer Meeting  | SU Council     | Leadership Training |                             |

*Delegation* enables us to lighten the load for ourselves, but also allows other people to have an involvement in ministry. Everybody recognises that it is quicker and easier to do it ourselves, but we must learn to train other people.

*Controlling the diary.* If we do not allocate specific time in our diary for a particular event, then that event is unlikely to take place.

*Handling interruptions.* We must deal politely, but firmly, with people whose demands on our time divert us from achieving the task. This, of course, means that we must be able to distinguish those who are genuinely seeking help from those who simply want to chat for an hour or two.

*Being decisive.* We need to learn not to make excuses for failing to take action to progress our goals.

*Handling paper.* This is recognised as a major problem, and people deal with it in different ways. Some, for example, set aside one day a month to deal with all correspondence, clear the desk etc.

*Learning to say 'No'.* Most of us recognise that we are not particularly good at this. The demands that people make upon our time are often legitimate, and the causes are good causes but, if we have committed time in our diary for family or leisure, then, except for emergencies, we should not allow that time to be taken by others.

## INVOLVING OTHERS

It is important for us to develop our own support system consisting of people we can trust, who will pray for us, and to whom we can turn when we have a particular problem or issue that needs to be talked through. This point, already made in earlier chapters, is important enough to be repeated.

We need to maintain strong and happy marriages. The benefits from a supportive home base are incalculable. Our problems often relate to the fact that our schedules are not synchronised with the schedules of our families. Children are at school during the day when we are at home; children are at home in the evening and at weekends when we are out. This can create pressures, and we need to devise strategies to overcome the difficulties.

It is also important for us to train our successor, and to have a team of people around us who will ensure that the priorities of the church are being met. This can create new problems, particularly in the early stages. We need to recognise that we are accountable to the other members of the team, and to recognise that they will have gifts different from ours. Ideally, all of the gifts required in a team should be represented—the visionary gifts, the implementation gifts, the interpersonal gifts, the finisher gifts. Our task is to build a team of people who will be able to provide the skills that we ourselves do not have.

CONCLUSION

If we are to keep on top of the job, we must deepen our knowledge both of God and of ourselves, and be much more willing to take decisions which will allow us greater control of our time. For our own sakes, and for the sake of the church, it is imperative that we find and maintain a joy and satisfaction in Christian service.

# 8

# Other Workers

## Neil Summerton

Most financially-supported workers in the local churches for whom this volume is intended are likely to be elders and to participate in the senior leadership of the congregation. This is because it is the teaching, pastoral and leadership roles that most naturally come to many people's minds when they think that their church needs full-time help. In practice, however, many FSWs in 'Brethren' and 'post-Brethren' churches do not fall into that category. Rather, they are often younger people, or women. They are not elders and are not seen by the congregation as included in the senior leadership. It is the special purpose of this chapter to consider the practical and other issues and difficulties which can influence the success of their ministry in the congregations using their services.

Such individuals are not a homogenous group, and it would be a mistake to treat them all alike. They can be of either sex. They can be of widely-varying age. Their roles can be very various, arising from the leaders' and the congregation's perceptions of the current needs of the church, and frequently arising from the particular gifts of the individual who, in effect, has volunteered for such service. It would not be an exhaustive list to note that there exist: evangelists, youth evangelists, youth workers, youth pastors, community workers, social workers, parents' and toddlers' workers, workers with the elderly, worship leaders, musical directors, administrators, secretaries, and exotic combinations of these different functions.

At times, too, the distinctions between such workers and 'ordinary' members of the congregation can become fuzzy. First, such FSWs may well in practice only be part-time and may have volunteer workers alongside them who have identical roles. Second, they may often have been 'ordinary' church members who, for the time being, have agreed to take on different or larger roles on a financially-supported basis, part-time or full-time. Such workers may shuttle backwards and forwards across the indistinct frontier between 'financially-supported workers' and 'ordinary' church members.

These types of church worker undoubtedly experience a number of special pressures and difficulties which are not necessarily shared by the superior category of FSW.

## STATUS AND ROLE

Perhaps the primary one is a set of pressures and difficulties which relate to the ambiguous status and role of such workers.

In the first chapter of this volume, I have referred to the risk that attitudes on the part of full-time leaders of congregations can encourage the emergence of a new, in effect 'clerical' class, with the full-time leaders marked off from both 'ordinary' members of the congregation and other congregational leaders, such as elders. It may come as a surprise to some to be told that the church workers with whom this chapter deals far too often find that they are treated by both congregations and full-time leaders as second-ranking full-time workers. They are second-class citizens, whose views, work and spiritual character are inferior to those of the first-ranking financially-supported workers. There is, of course, a double discrimination of this kind, for both religious and social reasons, where the worker concerned is a woman.

There is nothing particularly special about 'Brethren' and 'post-Brethren' churches in this respect. This discrimination, and the tendency towards stratification of status, seems to afflict all Christian congregations to a greater or lesser extent—try, for example, being a female religious in the Roman Catholic church. Given, however, the 'Brethren' ecclesiology which denies such distinctions of status between those who use their gifts for the benefit of the whole body, congregational leaders need to fight against it, both by teaching and by example.

## CHANGING STATUS AND ROLE

A further aspect of ambiguity of status and role grows specifically out of the present 'Brethren' and 'post-Brethren' context. It arises out of the fact that many churches appoint younger FSWs as a second-best course of action, or even with considerable reluctance.

Smaller congregations which are appointing someone for the first time are putting a cautious toe into the water. They doubt whether they can afford a senior leader. The latter would present accommodation problems which they cannot solve, whereas a younger single person will be able to rent accommodation without too much difficulty. They are reluctant to appoint someone from outside, whereas a younger person from the congregation is available. Larger, perhaps more traditional congregations are dubious about appointing a senior leader or elder full-time, perhaps because of the implications for those already in senior leadership. A younger person seems likely to rock the boat less and, in any case, can be given a specific area of responsibility, like youth work, that need not trouble the elders or the rest of the congregation too much—we want, of course, to see that youth work goes forward effectively, do we not?

Overarching all is the lack of a tradition of full-time work in these churches and the poor supply of suitable candidates from within the tradition. The congregations are forced to turn to the younger products of the Bible colleges and training institutes who certainly have not been trained for this type of congregation and may be unaware of the particular minefields into which they are moving.

Here is a pretty heady brew, and it is scarcely surprising that the results are sometimes explosive. It can be the more so where the younger worker is gifted and is leadership material, the more so still where they are female. They get stuck into the work with the enthusiasm and energy of youth. They begin to have some success, and gather round them a small, keen group of younger people. The congregation, and even the leadership, begin to look to them to take on more responsibility, here and there, because they are on the spot and there is no one else to take on the task. In any case, the elders have not really recognised or admitted to themselves that they appointed a youth worker, when what they really wanted/needed was an additional senior leader. The reality is that they recruited a full-time elder/leader on the cheap, and in the hope of not disturbing the dynamics of their existing, cosy leadership world.

The worker then begins to think how the congregational work, as well as their own work, could be developed. The elders don't seem very interested, perhaps because they lack the strategic appreciation that their young worker is gifted with. Communications between the elders and the worker are poor. The elders have made no specific arrangements for supervision. They do not invite the worker to their meetings regularly. The worker feels neglected and isolated. Self pity sets in. He or she does not react as maturely as desirable. He or she starts murmuring to their particular friends in the congregation. A distorted story gets back by a circuitous route to the elders. Relations begin to get more and more strained. It may all end in tears—bitter ones for the worker—and probably a bad conscience for the elders, if they have any perception and sensitivity.

Much of this results from the failure of the elders/senior leaders to be clear-eyed, in the beginning, about the needs of the fellowship, about what they were doing, about the need to make clear arrangements and to carry them through on a continuing basis. There is also frequently a failure to recognise that a young worker will almost inevitably develop and become more mature, constantly learning in the work. As that happens, the role needs to grow, and the relationship with the elders/senior leaders needs to grow and change with it. Elders also need to take a close interest in all FSWs, and to ensure that they enjoy proper supportive supervision and encouragement.

## TENSIONS BETWEEN SOCIAL WORK, AND EVANGELISTIC AND SPIRITUAL WORK

This third issue arises from the fact that it is frequently the case that younger FSWs are recruited for work which has an important social dimension. This may include work with young mothers and small children, children's work, youth clubs, community outreach and development work. The congregational leaders frequently see this as means to the end of extending the Kingdom in spiritual terms and of building up the congregation numerically. The worker, however, finds himself or herself inevitably and desirably drawn more and more into social work and action for its own sake. There are also professional and political pressures from the social work world to play down the spiritual and outreach dimensions of such work, and some have remarked[15] that, as a matter of observable fact, evangelistic and helping gifts are not commonly found in the same person. Soon the leaders can begin to ask where the spiritual results of the work are, and whether the worker is not concentrating too much on social work and not enough on outreach.

This is, of course, an old argument in 'Brethrenism', previously manifested in the tensions and divisions between those who considered that missionaries should concentrate on evangelism and church-planting, and those who considered that, for example, medical missionary work was unavoidable, and a desirable expression of the Kingdom of God for its own sake, and one that would lead in due course to the growth of the church. The tension can be a source of stress for younger FSWs.

For my part, I consider that church leaders need to see social action as a legitimate and practical expression by the local church

---

[15] E.g., Brian Hathaway, *Beyond Renewal. The Kingdom of God* , Word (U.K.)Ltd, 1990, pp 73,74.

of the Kingdom of God for its own sake; and be less rosy-eyed about the speed and directness with which 'spiritual' results will accrue from this type of work. And they should be careful not to upbraid their young FSWs for a situation which they ought to have expected anyway.

## ISSUES MORE PERSONAL TO THE WORKER, PARTICULARLY THOSE WHO ARE YOUNGER

There is a group of issues which are concerned with the very real emotional, psychological and practical pressures of the position, quite apart from those which result from the problems just discussed. Full-time Christian work is, in the eyes of wider society, a low-status activity, and so one of the normal sources of personal self-worth is closed off. It is also normally a poorly-paid activity, especially for the kind of worker referred to in this chapter. That imposes the pressures of seeking to make ends meet, as well as the temptation to rue the fact that many members of the congregation are better off than the younger FSW and yet, perhaps, expect the worker to live in poverty as a sign of spiritual virtue in those thus devoted to the Lord. It is, therefore, an inherently insecure role, both emotionally and practically.

This is exacerbated by the pressures deriving from the real or imagined expectations of the congregation and the leadership as to what the worker will achieve. There can be the constant nagging fear that the congregation are making sacrifices to pay the worker, yet there is nothing to show for it in return by way of growth. This may be entirely in the mind of the worker; but on occasion such suspicion as to what the congregation are thinking may well be fully justified.

The result may be a drive to achieve, at the expense of long working-hours, constant effort, and detriment to family and social life. That, in turn, may lead to loneliness and isolation, which may in any case be the natural experience of a FSW in a congregation in which most members, including the leaders, have full-time jobs which prevent contact with the FSW during working hours.

Recognition of these emotional, psychological and practical pressures should alert the congregational leadership to the need for proper supervision and pastoral care of its FSWs, particularly the younger ones.

## PRACTICAL ARRANGEMENTS

A number of practical arrangements should be put in place to ensure that there is adequate supervision and care. To a considerable extent, it is a question of applying good personnel practice with which most of us are familiar from the secular context. These include the following:

## GOOD, EASY COMMUNICATIONS BETWEEN THE WORKER AND THE ELDERS

This is an absolute essential. It should be the norm for the worker to meet with the elders every three months or so, to discuss the progress of the work, and to consider any problems, both in terms of the work and of a practical nature for the worker. One of the elders should be identified as a channel of communication with the elders that the worker can use at any time to communicate with the elders in an informal and relaxed way. It needs to be someone who is reasonably accessible (e.g., not absent abroad on business half the time), and who is, above all, conscientious and in sympathy with the worker and the work that is being undertaken.

## EFFECTIVE MANAGERIAL SUPERVISION

This should probably be undertaken by the same person. It will require close knowledge of the work on the part of the supervisor, accessibility, and regular meetings on a one-to-one basis, to discuss how the work is going, consider problems, and act as a guide and mentor without removing responsibility for the work from the worker. The role requires tact, but also firmness when necessary, for example, if the worker is in practice sloppy or lax, or is showing signs of workaholism.

## JOB DESCRIPTION AND PERSONAL OBJECTIVES AND TARGETS

The manager should certainly see that the worker draws up a job description and personal objectives and targets, at least annually, and that these receive the approval of the eldership group as a whole. Progress against the objectives and targets should be reviewed regularly with the worker by the managerial supervisor, not to lash the worker, but because we all find this regular discipline helpful and reassuring in our work, if it is carried out in the right spirit.

## FINANCIAL AND ACCOMMODATION ISSUES

The managerial supervisor should be on the look-out for any practical, financial and accommodation problems that the worker may have, so as to try to anticipate them, rather than seeking to deal with them only when they have become a serious source of distraction, pressure and anxiety.

## TRAINING AND PROFESSIONAL DEVELOPMENT

The managerial supervisor should also have an eye to the training and professional development of the worker. Young workers should not be allowed to vegetate in an easy niche. They should be expected to develop and add to their skills and expertise, and even prepare to branch off in a new direction with growing maturity. They should certainly be allowed some time for appropriate formal training and personal development activities, and it should be the responsibility of the managerial supervisor to see that arrangements are made and acted upon.

## PROFESSIONAL SUPERVISOR

It may well be the case, of course, that the supervising elder is not an expert in the particular type of work that the worker is doing, particularly if it is of a social or community work nature. In those circumstances, it may be that the worker should also have a professional supervisor whom he or she sees from time to time, say, once every six months, to obtain professional guidance. In that case, the elders should remember that it is normal to pay for such professional supervision!

## SEPARATE PASTORAL CARE ARRANGEMENTS

The good manager recognises, of course, that there is an important pastoral dimension to management—that of guiding, encouraging and leading, based on sympathetic understanding of the person being managed, the work they are doing, and the pressures and difficulties to which it gives rise. But in the context of Christian work in the local church, there is a case for separate pastoral care arrangements for the worker. The managerial supervisor may, from time to time, have to 'manage'—that is, to exercise a fairly strong hand in the interests of the work, the congregation and the elders, and this may interfere with the pastoral relationship. Pastoral care by someone outside that relationship may be helpful, as long as the pastor does not seek to try to interfere with, or duplicate, the managerial supervisor's work. They must also both guard against the worker's trying to manipulate and play one off against the other. The same is true of the professional supervisor who should have a strictly advisory, not managerial, role in respect of the worker.

## SUPPORT GROUP OF PEERS

The worker may well benefit from a small support group of peers with whom to meet regularly for prayer. This can have a valuable pastoral function.

These are the kind of practical arrangements that need, in my view, to be made in order to ensure that the younger FSWs are properly cared for and managed by the congregational leaders who have appointed them. Given the 'Brethren' tradition, the elders should be especially careful to ensure that female FSWs receive quality care and management. Social and religious tradition in this respect tends to think that women can simply be neglected because they are, after all, 'only women'.

## RELATIONSHIPS BETWEEN FINANCIALLY-SUPPORTED WORKERS

A final question that arises is the relationship between the younger FSW(s) and the senior FSW in the same church, who is also an elder. Should they form a separate team under the leadership and management of the senior worker?

It is doubtful whether one should be prescriptive about this. Much will depend on circumstances, and on the character of the workers, and their gifts. There will, of course, be a natural tendency in this direction, since they will probably meet frequently in the course of the week, and talk and perhaps work together. But there are dangers, especially in the 'Brethren' context.

It would be very easy for the FSWs to develop into a separate 'staff' team, distinct from the (rest of) the elders, and viewed differently from them by the congregation and the FSWs themselves. There is a risk, too, that it would reinforce the trend towards the professionalisation of ministry, the development of a practical 'clergy', and the hobbling of the wide exercise of gift in the congregation.

Everything depends on the particular circumstances but, in my judgment, it is probably best if managerial supervision of younger FSWs is carried out by an elder who is not financially-supported by the congregation.

# 9

# Orientation to the 'Brethren' Scene

Harold Rowdon
*Author of* The Origins of the Brethren

One of the most striking features of the contemporary church scene is the development of what might be called 'evangelical convergence'. Though some evangelicals retain their denominational or theological distinctives almost unchanged, an increasing number are moving away from rigidly held positions and sometimes find themselves sharing common views.

An increasing number of 'non-Brethren' churches are becoming less denominationally minded and more local church orientated. The distinction between clergy and laity is being narrowed. Ordination is losing some of its mystique and baptism is sometimes seen as a kind of ordination to service. Team leadership is becoming the norm. The Lord's Supper is becoming more central in churches where it used to be little more than an optional extra. The widespread use of spiritual gifts is more commonly allowed and even encouraged.

If 'non-Brethren' churches are becoming more like 'Brethren' ones, a growing number of 'Brethren' churches are changing in such a way as to make for convergence from their side. Without sacrificing the local church focus (in some cases strengthening it), they are building working relationships with other local churches of any or no denomination, particularly if they are evangelical. The need for churches to enjoy the service of leaders working full-time is being realised more widely. Alongside this, it is gradually being accepted that endowment with spiritual gifts, particularly when they are being exercised in a full-time ministry, can hardly fail to create distinctions, and even differences, between church members. In a handful of cases a clergy/laity divide appears to be emerging. Again, the nature of public worship is being reassessed as a result of growing concern over the dominating influence of the Breaking of Bread which, while it has kept 'Brethren' worship Christocentric has often prevented it from being fully theocentric, and has not infrequently degenerated from what was commonly called 'Spirit-led' worship into something little more than the mouthing of platitudes and the parroting of time-honoured liturgical formulae.

Our purpose here is not to develop the scenario further, but to use it as a backdrop for a consideration of underlying 'Brethren' distinctives, inasfar as they relate to full-time ministry in a local church situation. We will then go on to consider some of the changes that have been taking places in a small but growing number of Brethren churches. After noting some areas of possible tension which can easily appear when 'non-Brethren' undertake full-time ministry in a church which has a 'Brethren' background, we shall conclude by suggesting some ways in which these tensions can be eased.

## 'BRETHREN' ARE EVANGELICALS

Even a thumbnail sketch of 'Brethren' should start by pointing out that they are recognisably evangelical. If by 'evangelical' we mean, with John Stott, that they are 'Bible people' and 'Gospel people', or, with David Bebbington, that they are Bible-centred and Cross-centred, that they insist on the need for conversion and are tirelessly activist, then 'Brethren' pass the test with flying colours. Their dedication to the Bible and the Gospel is almost unequalled among evangelicals, and their activity, particularly in evangelism, is prodigious.

## 'BRETHREN' ARE MORE THAN EVANGELICALS

'Brethren' distinctives, however, go far beyond those of other evangelicals. Actually, in their very early days 'Brethren' reacted *against* many aspects of church life common among evangelicals, such as insistence on an ordained ministry, the virtual silencing of the laity in church, and such regard for their particular church tradition as to give it an authority almost equal to that of scripture. The reaction went to such lengths as to give 'Brethren' the appearance of a sect—if not a cult—despite their counterbalancing theme of the unity of all (true) believers in Christ. In a memorable phrase, one of the founders of the Evangelical Alliance, Angell James, a leading Congregationalist divine, included the 'Plymouth Brethren' with 'Papists' and 'Puseyites' as opponents of evangelicals!

Some strands of 'Brethren' teaching provide some justification for such a view. One example is the incredible theory enunciated by J N Darby that the church has been 'in ruins' ever since apostolic times, that it has been rejected by God as a formal structure, and that any attempt to create a church structure is not only misguided but a mark of apostasy. All that is left for the faithful in such a situation is to meet as 'two or three', claiming the promise that Jesus would be in their midst, and obeying his command to break bread in remembrance of him. While those known as 'Open Brethren' do not subscribe to this view, there are indications that they have not been entirely unaffected by it.

Less extreme—and widely accepted by evangelicals who are not 'Brethren', particularly in North America—is the dispensationalist approach to scripture. This includes the assertion that a sharp contrast exists between Israel, God's earthly people, and the church, his heavenly people. When Israel rejected Jesus as her earthly Messiah, he turned to a new task—that of becoming the spiritual Saviour of the world by laying down his life as an atoning sacrifice. Following his resurrection and ascension, the Holy Spirit was given on the Day of Pentecost and the process began of gathering out, from Jews and Gentiles alike, a heavenly people as his church. When this process is complete he will return, in two stages, first to 'rapture' the complete church to heaven, and then, after seven years of unprecedented persecution directed against the Jews, to save his earthly people in their extremity and to set up the earthly kingdom promised to them in the Old Testament. This 'dispensationalist' approach to scripture has had a much longer life among 'Open Brethren'.than the 'church in ruins' theory, though today, in UK, it is held lightly—if at all—among all but the most traditional 'Brethren'.

One other extreme reaction should be mentioned. This was a reductionist view of the humanity of Jesus which came close to and sometimes slipped over the boundary into formal heresy. In their anxiety not to besmirch the divine nature of the incarnate Son of God, some 'Brethren' underestimated the 'earthly' nature of his humanity, even using the term 'heavenly humanity'.[16] Though this view has had little currency, except among some of the 'Exclusive Brethren' groups, it has left its mark remarkably widely in a largely unconscious playing down of the real humanity of Jesus. Many 'Brethren' speak and write as if the human feet of Jesus barely touched the ground!

Twentieth-century 'Brethren' need not feel unduly embarrassed by such eccentricities. Most religious movements (including the early church) have produced them. In most cases, including the

---

[16]   For further details, see the fascinating article by F F Bruce on 'The humanity of Jesus Christ', in *The Journal of the Christian Brethren Research Fellowship*, Number 24, September 1973.

'Brethren' (particularly the 'Open' variety), they have eventually fallen away, or at least have lost their rough edges.

Close attention does need to be given, however, to a number of distinctives which characterize, to a greater or lesser degree, mainstream 'Brethren' thought and practice.

## ATTITUDE TO THE BIBLE

Protestants in general and evangelicals in particular have been described as 'people of the book'. This is particularly—almost uniquely—true of the 'Brethren'. From their inception, they have revered the Bible as God's Word, divinely inspired, uniquely authoritative and absolutely trustworthy. Their respect for it has made many of them reluctant to place any object on top of a printed copy of it! They read it, on their own and in family devotions (though perhaps not universally, as was once the case). They study it, sometimes in the original languages, and with the aid of concordances and commentaries. They expound it in public, and they use it in their evangelism. An astonishing number of 'Brethren' have become university professors in biblical and related studies. F F Bruce was only one of half a dozen or more. Curiously, the Bible has not been used as much as might have been expected in their public worship. Perhaps this was because their worship was so largely patterned on that portrayed in 1 Corinthians 11–14 (minus the 'extraordinary' gifts of the Spirit).

'Brethren' have been particularly fond of the allegorical method of interpreting scripture. This is by no means unique among evangelicals, though it was at one time almost a 'Brethren' hallmark. It may well have some connection with their passionate devotion to the person of Christ, for it has enabled them to find him in Old Testament 'types', in the minutest details of the Tabernacle and in even less likely places.

Being human, there are curious inconsistencies among latter-day 'Brethren'. Although professing to be thoroughly biblical and to have no regard for man-made tradition, they have nevertheless allowed their own traditions to develop to a point where they possess an authority which sometimes actually undermines that of scripture. Vocal when scripture is silent, and silent when scripture is vocal, often resting on the merest scrap of biblical evidence or boldest inference from biblical practice, 'Brethren' tradition may, in fact, be devoid of real scriptural warrant. Yet it will be defended passionately. You may cite as many passages of scripture as you like in support of your contention, but if they can quote a single passage which appears to them to justify their position, they will ignore you.

They may even reply, as someone once did to me in the heat of the moment: 'I don't mind what scripture says . . .'.

Another peculiarity is that traditional Brethren imagine that, just as the Old Testament provided detailed instructions for the Tabernacle and all that went on inside it, so the New Testament gives full specifications for the religious life of the Christian. What made them imagine this is difficult to discover, but it is a deeply rooted 'tradition'. In an increasing number of churches, however, it is being realised that the New Testament provides basic principles which must be embodied in forms appropriate to the prevailing culture; precedents, not all of which were normative; but not a detailed pattern to be followed everywhere and for all time.

## VIEWS OF THE CHURCH

'Brethren' distinctives concerning the church largely revolve around two focal points—the local church and the universal church. With regard to the former they stress the autonomy of each local church, although in practice this is not absolute since, for example, most 'Brethren' churches are reluctant to step out of line with the others. As to the latter, they are firmly wedded to the view that **all** true believers belong to the one church of which Christ is the head, although in practice they rarely give tangible expression to this belief.

In the area between these two focal points, 'Brethren' tend to be ambivalent. Some—at both ends of the traditional/non traditional spectrum—deny that they form part of any distinctive group of churches, i.e., 'The Brethren'. 'We are merely groups of Christian believers', they say, 'meeting in the way we feel to be most biblical and appropriate'. Those at the more traditional end of the spectrum find it difficult, if not impossible, to relate to denominational churches since they feel unable to recognize them as valid churches.[17] The others, however, are prepared to accept individual churches as valid expressions of New Testament Christianity, though they may have difficulty in recognising the validity of denominational usages of the word 'church'.[18]

---

[17] In this connection, it is worth remembering that 'Brethren' declined to use customary terms, such as 'church', 'service', 'sermon' and 'offering', replacing them with the neutral ones 'hall', 'assembly', 'meeting', 'address' and 'collection', respectively.

[18] For a powerful presentation of the view that churches of any or no denomination may be recognized as the modern equivalent of NT 'household churches', see H L Ellison's remarkable little book, *The Household Church*, Paternoster Press, 1963.

## LEADERSHIP PATTERNS

Today's 'Brethren' have inherited a view of the ministry which once, as we have seen, made them evangelical pariahs, but is now being widely 'discovered' by other evangelicals and even by some non-evangelicals. 'Brethren' have always passionately opposed any sharp distinction between 'clergy' and 'laity', rightly pointing out that, in biblical usage, *laos* means the people of God as a whole. Equally forcefully, they proclaimed—and put into practice—New Testament teaching on the widespread distribution of spiritual gifts within the Body of Christ (though their unperceived cultural conditioning caused them to confine this to those of male gender and to restrict the range of spiritual gifts expected).

Whereas 'Exclusive Brethren' abjured all forms of leadership structure of a formal kind, while submitting to various species of informal leadership patterns which were all the more powerful for being unrecognised, 'Open Brethren' have been much less inhibited. Some, however, who have been directly or indirectly influenced by 'Exclusive' views, have been reluctant to give much recognition to their leaders. There may still be a few 'assemblies' where leadership is the responsibility of a 'brothers' meeting'. In theory, any 'brother' is entitled to attend such a meeting, though it is usually assumed that only those will attend who feel qualified to do so. Slightly advanced on this is the situation where a group of men, which is self-perpetuating, described as 'brethren in oversight', or 'the oversight', meet to discuss and take decisions on matters affecting the church.

Particularly since the 1950s and '60s, there has been a considerable increase in the number of 'Brethren' churches which recognize elders (there have always been some), and also a sub-group of deacons to attend to the more mundane issues. The authority of the elders may be considerable. Rarely are they in any meaningful sense accountable to the church, though in recent years a small but growing number of churches have devised means whereby the views of church members are taken into account when appointing elders.

In general, church meetings are seen by 'Brethren' as occasions for reporting to the church, both by the elders and by leaders of sectional activities, and for 'sensing' the mood of the church. Decision-making is not seen as appropriate, and any suggestion of voting is usually condemned outright as an attempt to introduce 'democracy' into the church.[19] The opinions of church members on matters of substantial importance to the church may be sought in more informal and less public ways (e.g., by correspondence).

## MINISTRY

Almost without realising it, 'Brethren' have enjoyed a form of ministry that could be described as 'apostolic' if not 'episcopal'. Gifted men were recognised in an informal but significant way as exercising an itinerant ministry which took them around the country, and, in many cases, around the world. Some functioned as evangelists; others as Bible teachers whose ministry was rarely—if ever—questioned. These latter served the function of helping to create the near uniformity of belief and practice which made 'Brethren' the tightly knit 'denomination' which it became (unacknowledged though that was!)

True, there were mavericks—men of independent judgment like G H Lang and H L Ellison who were prepared to question generally accepted shibboleths. Moreover, 'Brethren' were never monochrome (if you look hard enough you can find exceptions to almost any generalisation made about them). But the ministry of Bible teachers—written as well as oral, given in books and magazines as well as in Bible teaching conferences—created a high degree of homogeneity.[20]

## WORSHIP

Traditional 'Brethren' worship is highly distinctive. It may well have been influenced almost as much by Quaker practice as by 1 Corinthians 11–14, and the central place it gives to the Lord's Table may owe something to the high church background of several of the 'Brethren' founding fathers.

'Brethren' worship consists almost entirely of 'what happens around the Lord's Table'. For some reason, 'Brethren' had a

---

[19]   I sometimes wonder why those who believe it is biblical to trust the Holy Spirit to guide open worship are so horrified at the thought of trusting him to guide the church in decision making. (Perhaps it has something to do with the founding fathers' hostility to anything savouring of secular democracy, living as they did under the shadow of the French Revolution—though the resemblance to democracy is illusory.)

[20]   'Exclusive Brethren' (and, at one stage, even 'Open Brethren') went as far as to use the term 'accredited ministry'—though accredited by whom is not very clear! Herein lay one of the most potent seeds of the mid-twentieth-century Taylorite débacle.

passion for putting things into neat packages! So, worship took place on Sunday mornings, gospel preaching on Sunday evenings, Bible study and prayer on weeknights. Even worship, I was once told by a traditionalist, must not be confused with hymn singing, or prayer, or Bible ministry. In my confusion, I asked what worship **was**, but did not receive a coherent answer!

So, worship takes place at the Lord's Table. It takes the form of spontaneous, or, rather, Spirit-led, contributions along the lines of 1 Corinthians 14:26—minus the revelations, prophecies, tongues and interpretations which, according to the standard dispensationalist view, are no longer given. Presumably because 1 Corinthians 11:17ff is immediately followed by 1 Corinthians 12 to 14, the symbols on the Lord's Table set the agenda for worship. As a result, 'Brethren' worship focuses primarily—sometimes exclusively—on the death of Christ, or at the very most his person and work.

Perhaps because of the atmosphere of solemnity, seriousness, and a degree of silence, as well as the awe-inspiring and sobering nature of its content, 'Brethren' worship is marked by often undetected emotional intensity as well as spiritual fervour. Although professedly directed towards God and designed to exalt him, in practice it may also be an experience which is emotionally exhilarating to the worshipper. Often described by those who practise is as 'precious', it is likely to be jealously guarded against any significant alteration.

Lying at the heart of 'Brethren' spirituality is a devotion to the person of Christ which is exceedingly deep. To an almost unequalled degree, 'Brethren' have entered into the 'mystical' as well as the intellectual side of the teaching of Paul about being 'in Christ' and being identified with him. Their 'love affair' with Christ has generated extraordinary devotion to him which has found expression in worship which focuses upon him and upon his cross as the most vivid and appealing revelation of his love for them. It has also motivated them to contend for the truth about him, to proclaim him to others as Saviour and Lord, to take the gospel to the four corners of the earth, and to look forward eagerly to his return.

Despite its deep sincerity, 'Brethren' worship has obvious deficiencies. It almost ignores the Father, and completely bypasses the Holy Spirit.[21] It can become unhealthily introspective and almost obsessively emotional. Nor is it exempt from the tendency of any liturgical pattern (however informal) to become repetitive, mechanical, and enervating.

---

[21] This stricture does not apply to the 'Taylorite Brethren'.

## BAPTISM

As far as 'Open Brethren' are concerned, believers are the only fit subjects for Christian baptism (though some 'Exclusive' groups practise 'household baptism'). They enjoy a rich theology of baptism, seeing it not only as an act of obedience, but as symbolising identification with Christ in his death, burial, and resurrection. As part of initiation, some have associated it with conversion and entry into the church universal rather than into a local church. Today, most 'Open Brethren' would not hold this view, though many would not see it as necessarily leading immediately to church membership.[22]

A vexed question is whether baptism is a condition for church membership. Those who may be described as 'purists' maintain that it is, and that any form of baptism other than total immersion as believers is invalid. Others, following George Müller, take the view that, while baptism as a believer is the norm, saving faith in Christ is the sole condition of salvation. Therefore it is possible to be a true believer without having been baptised as such (like the penitent thief on the cross). George Müller's aphorism that the only indispensable condition for church membership, as for salvation, is 'life', not 'light', is widely accepted. While the scriptural norm is seen to be the baptism of believers, appeal is often made to Mark 16:16 as justifying a soft rather than a hard attitude on this matter. Some would accept the validity of infant baptism, conversion, and confirmation **in that order**, and a few might go even further and not expect someone converted after becoming a full member in a paedobaptist church to undergo believer's baptism.

## WORLDLINESS

One other distinctive, which is not absolutely distinctive but which is essential for an understanding of the 'Brethren mind' is the traditional attitude adopted towards 'the world'. 'Brethren' are not alone in regarding 'the world' (i.e., the human environment in which we live) as alien, hostile, and all but barred to the Christian, but few evangelicals have implemented that attitude so vigorously.

While continuing to live in the world, 'Brethren' traditionally sought the maximum of independence from it. Without following the path of self-denying asceticism for very long, they have, until recently, reduced their links with the world to a bare minimum.

---

[22]  A surprising number of 'Open Brethren' churches have no clearly defined membership. This probably stems from the desire not to create 'denominational' barriers between themselves and other true believers living in the neighbourhood.

Apart from involvement in education (though they did set up a number of their own schools) and in gainful employment (in which they often achieved outstanding success), they lived an almost completely segregated existence. 'Assembly life' provided an almost complete round of activities, fulfilling almost every recognised human social need. Association with non-Christians was minimal. The world of entertainment was strictly out of bounds. The use of alcohol was often (though not always) forbidden, along with tobacco, cosmetics, almost all jewellery and blatantly fashionable clothes. When holidaymaking came into wider use, 'Brethren' took the lead in setting up Christian 'guesthouses' where Christians could avoid mixing socially with non-Christians. Politics, both local and national, were commonly regarded as inappropriate for Christians (though several 'Brethren' served with some distinction as mayors of towns and Members of Parliament).

The early 'Brethren' tendency towards asceticism, and the more tenacious 'separation' from the world no longer characterise the less traditional 'Open Brethren'. (In recent decades the latter has been carried by the 'Taylorite Brethren to extremes which have become scandalous.)

We have done little more than skim the surface, but we must move on to consider some of the changes which have taken place among the 'Brethren' during the last few decades. Churches which are likely to avail themselves of 'financially-supported workers' are almost certain to have experienced some or all of these (though, as I have already indicated, they may nevertheless still bear some of the marks of traditional 'Brethrenism').

## CHANGES IN LEADERSHIP PATTERNS

Attention has already been drawn to the post-World War II trend to recognise elders and deacons as church leaders. Initially, elders functioned as general leaders, discussing and taking decisions on the full range of local church affairs. When they realised that the pressing financial, practical concerns tended to crowd out pastoral matters from the limited time at their disposal, the leadership of a growing number of 'Brethren' churches has delegated to a group of deacons responsibility for practical matters. Usually some system of linkage between elders and deacons has been put in place to ensure coordination (and, it must be added, ultimate control by the elders).

The next important change has been the appointment of one (occasionally more than one) person (usually male) to devote his or her full time to church work. The major reason for this has been the perceived inability of a group of men who are usually engaged full-time in employment under modern conditions to devote enough time to their church responsibilities as elders. Pastoral, administrative, evangelistic, and social ministries have suffered in consequence. It may also be that the analogy with overseas missionary work has played a part in bringing about this change. Many missionaries have spent their full time planting churches, pastoring congregations, discipling new believers, teaching and training church members, often with results that put UK 'Brethren' to shame. Even in the UK, it is not a totally new development. There have been precedents from the very beginning of the movement, such as Robert Chapman and George Müller, and there have been isolated instances subsequently. More importantly, there are biblical precedents (e.g., Paul at Ephesus).

It was easier for 'Brethren' churches to appoint evangelists in this way, and some surprisingly traditional churches have done so. But from the '70s and '80s men have been called to full-time local ministry as pastors and teachers, as well as youth workers and community workers. In some cases, women have been appointed similarly, though rarely as pastors or teachers.

One further development has followed. In a small but growing number of churches, the suitability of elders and deacons as the leadership pattern has been questioned. Practical problems have raised the question. It may have been difficult to find sufficient men of the calibre required to fulfil the very exacting requirements of the office of elder. There may have been dissatisfaction with a system which entrusts to what is effectively a self-perpetuating oligarchy a huge degree of authority and power over the entire life of the church, including the power of veto over the decisions of those men and women who are the actual leaders of sectional activities (for children, youth, women, etc). There may have been cultural problems, too. At a time when business management takes place at various levels, and when the distinction between management and workforce is less sharp than it was, the plausibility of a highly authoritarian command structure is being called into question.

At the crucial biblical level, attention has been drawn to a number of neglected factors. These include the following. There was diversity of leadership structures in New Testament churches (cf. Jerusalem with Antioch, Corinth and Crete). The fact that Paul enjoined Timothy and Titus to appoint elders and deacons does not necessarily make such an arrangement binding for all time. If it did, there are serious omissions: for example, nothing is said about the duties of deacons nor about the procedure for choosing future elders and deacons. The crucial thing, it is being realised, is that leaders should embody New Testament *principles* of leadership, whatever nomenclature or job description is given them.

An increasing number of 'Brethren' churches are therefore experimenting with various kinds of leadership team, usually—but not invariably—retaining elders, and often including women.

This is not the place to debate the vexed question of the role of women in the church, though there are clear biblical precedents and principles in support, as well as historical precedents. This much, however, must be said: leaving on one side for the moment the question of gender, if the issue of leadership is approached from the angle of spiritual gifts, the position is clear. If God has gifted believers, female as well as male, for leadership then there can be no objection about providing suitable opportunities for exercising those gifts.

## NEW FORMS OF WORSHIP

There has been a marked tendency, for some years now, to move away from exclusively cross-centred, even Christ-centred worship, to worship which is God-centred. By no means does this exclude or minimise the importance of focusing on Christ and his cross. What it seeks to do is to achieve a full-orbed worship which does justice to biblical teaching and practice.

This has led to the introduction of more exuberant styles of worship utilising new forms of musical accompaniment,[23] and spirited as well as some restrained worship songs of modern vintage. As to content, this has widened to include exaltation of God in all that the Bible reveals about him and in all that the worshippers have experienced of his grace. Interestingly, one consequence of this has been that greater use has been made of the Bible in worship, including Bible exposition.

This transition from the old to the new has almost always been difficult, and often painful. Traditional 'Brethren' worship' (as described earlier in this chapter) is one thing. Joyful, exultant praise of God is another. Many churches have found that to introduce the second into the same service almost destroys the first, and the tendency has been to re-time and restyle worship altogether. It has often proved helpful to introduce a degree of set structure into the worship, with someone deputed to provide a lead. Usually—though not always—an element of free, unstructured participation has been preserved.

---

[23] The unaccompanied worship of yesteryear has vanished from all but the most traditional 'Open Brethren' churches.

Two other major changes in corporate worship must be mentioned, though neither can be elaborated. A growing number of churches are allowing—and, indeed, encouraging—women to participate in worship; and a smaller but not insignificant number are giving freedom for the use—under proper controls—of the full range of spiritual gifts. In both cases this is done, not in defiance of scripture, but in the belief that, in the past, scripture has been misunderstood and misapplied. It may be that there is a previously undetected flexibility in scripture which gives authenticity to practices in one cultural setting which may not be appropriate in another. It is undeniable that cultural changes in secular society have helped to bring about the changes just mentioned, though I would prefer to say that cultural changes have *alerted* us to elements in biblical teaching which, hitherto, have been overlooked (cf. the changing attitude of Christians towards slavery). Let us not overlook the undoubted fact that the practices of earlier 'Brethren', like those of almost all nineteenth-century evangelicals, were conditioned by *their* cultural background.

As for the emergence of full-blown 'charismatic' worship in 'Brethren' churches, this is a sea-change. Until perhaps ten years ago, anyone in a 'Brethren' church who showed the slightest inclination towards 'charismatic' practices was required to leave— and in this way the charismatic movement was provided with some of its finest leaders! During the past decade,however, the number of 'Brethren' churches which have embraced some or all of the practices commonly known as 'charismatic' and have remained within the broad ambit of 'Brethren' churches has steadily grown, though some have linked up with charismatic groupings. The number of those which have become fully 'charismatic' may be less than twenty, but a much larger number permit, if not encourage, the use of a wider range of spiritual gifts in worship than has been customary in 'Brethren' churches, and many more use modern 'worship songs'.

## NEW-STYLE EVANGELISM

'Brethren' evangelism has traditionally relied on a 'gospel meeting' each Sunday night, supplemented by 'missions' lasting a week or a fortnight, led by full-time evangelists. In addition, full-time evangelists have engaged in pioneer evangelism, mainly in rural areas, as a result of which numerous churches have been planted. The results of all this over the years have been very considerable. For some time now, however, it has been apparent that the results have become negligible. Nevertheless—no doubt in part at least

because of the development of a strong 'maintenance mentality'—
the routine has continued, particularly as far as the gospel meeting
is concerned.

Not a moment too soon, however, the Sunday evening 'gospel
meeting' has been abandoned in a considerable number of 'Brethren' churches. The discovery was made that—in some areas—people are more prepared to attend Sunday morning worship,
particularly if they can come as a family, and so the formal outreach
activity has been moved from Sunday evening to Sunday morning.
Usually known as a 'family service', the first part of the service
focuses on the children present, before they leave for teaching
classes (though in at least one case this is reversed, with the adults
leaving and the children—who form the bulk of that particular
congregation—remaining for the rest of their service).

The change from 'gospel meeting' to 'family service' involves
even more dramatic change. The traditional 'gospel meeting' was
virtually confrontational in tone, with the 'outsiders' present being
targeted not only in the preaching but even, in some instances, in
the prayers and hymns. In sharp contrast, the 'family service ' is
usually designed as a service of Christian worship in which those
who are not Christians can participate as far as they are able, and
through which they will be encouraged to become Christians.
Sometimes, an evangelistic note will be struck, and in one case
known to me, the gospel will occasionally be proclaimed by means
of a carefully structured 'communion service' in which all who are
believers are invited to take part.

[As an indication of the speed of cultural change today, some
churches are beginning to question the value of this kind of 'family'
service, since an increasing number of people no longer experience
'family' life, and find the concept of a 'family service' distasteful.]

The evangelistic mission, lasting for a week or a fortnight and
consisting mainly of nightly gospel preaching has also been abandoned very generally. The forty or so evangelists linked together in
the network known as 'Counties' (formerly 'Counties Evangelistic
Work') have long since ceased, by and large, to rely on 'missions'
and have developed new evangelistic strategies. These include a
professionally designed Bible Exhibition.

## RETURN TO SOCIAL ACTION

One of the greatest hindrances to effective evangelism in the past
has been the isolation of 'Brethren' from their non-Christian
contemporaries, and one of the greatest weaknesses in their presentation of the love of God has been the almost complete absence

of any tangible evidence of it in action, apart from the enthusiastic use of words.

Both these matters have been addressed in recent years by the same process—developing ways of helping various categories of people in need. The idea of helping people with needs other than 'spiritual' is not totally new to 'Brethren'. There is evidence that, in the nineteenth century, they were prepared to set up institutions like soup kitchens. More recently, from the 1940s, activities for children and young people, such as 'youth centres' and youth camps, made provision for physical and recreational as well as spiritual needs. In recent years, the inability of the Welfare State to deliver everything that has been expected of it has provided an opportunity for voluntary bodies to fill the gaps—and the state has welcomed this. A small but increasing number of 'Brethren' churches have been prepared to make use of their resources in terms of plant, personnel, and expertise, to run mothers' and toddlers' groups, luncheon clubs for the elderly, recreational activities for the retired, and even enquiry centres to advise those bewildered by bureaucracy and to help the unemployed to find work.

Fear of the 'social gospel' causes some to be wary of such things, but they have proved to be ways in which God's love can be demonstrated and 'bridges into the community' constructed.

## CHANGES IN ATTITUDES TO THE WORLD

One further area of change should be mentioned. Almost imperceptibly, attitudes towards the cultural environment in which we live have begun to alter. The words of Jesus about **not** taking his people out of the world but keeping them **in** it have been taken at face value. The walls behind which most 'Brethren' sheltered from the world have been lowered, and in consequence some have been able to serve as salt as well as light in society. The dangers are considerable, but so is the potential for commending the gospel, extending the kingdom, and giving practical expression to the love of God. *Involvement* need not result in *entanglement*.

With all this in mind, what are the areas of tension likely to arise consequent upon the introduction of someone from another church background to work full-time in a 'Brethren' environment?

## ROUTINE TENSIONS

Some tensions may arise in any case, quite apart from those arising from this particular circumstance. These include lack of clear terms of engagement, failure to respect them if they have been agreed, rigid adherence to them when it should be obvious that they require amending in the light of a developing situation. Or they may result from difficulties in personal relationships, sometimes amounting to personality clashes. Lack of gift and ability in the worker and/or others involved is another example. These are dealt with in other contributions to this volume.

Another kind of routine tension arises from failure to appreciate the complexities involved in the management of change. But, though this could arise in the case of *any* full-time church worker, it may well be exacerbated in the case of someone who does not appreciate the peculiarities of the situation in a church with 'Brethren' roots.

This is the nub of the matter, and we must turn to it.

## TENSIONS ARISING FROM BEING UNAWARE OF THE PECULIARITIES OF THE SITUATION

These arise from the fact that someone from another church tradition is undertaking a role—and a key one at that—which is likely to be new and untried. That person comes with presuppositions and expectations—not all of them conscious—which may differ markedly from those possessed by some or all of the people whom he or she has come to serve. They will all be treading a road which is new to them. There would be teething troubles even if everyone concerned came from the same background. How much more when this is not the case.

A variety of specific tensions may arise. Some of the most fundamental will be in the area of relationships between existing leaders and the one who has been brought in, full-time, to fill a completely new role. In most cases, the existing leaders will be known as elders, and will exercise a role which gives them very extensive powers. But they are only available for limited amounts of time—they are really 'part-time' elders. The introduction of someone who will be more available to people, who will almost certainly be trained for the task, and may be more gifted than some, at least, of the existing elders, is bound to affect the position of the latter. They may feel that they are being sidelined.

The position will not be helped if the full-time worker is placed in the category of someone in full-time employment, since, consciously or not, the original elders may view themselves as his or her employer. It will be worsened if, as sometimes happens, the worker is not recognised as one of the elders. This may not matter if the person is working as a community or youth worker, but if his or her work is indistinguishable from that of an elder, it is likely to create difficulties.

Tensions may also arise in specific areas of church life. The importance traditionally attached to the 'Breaking of Bread' may not be appreciated by someone from a church tradition which does not bestow equal importance on the ordinance. Even though this emphasis may have been moderated in practice, there will almost certainly be a number of people in the church who maintain it vigorously and will not appreciate the presence in their midst—and in a leading role—of someone who does not appear to share it.

Perhaps even more important is the traditional 'Brethren' distaste for anything savouring of 'one-man ministry'. This is something which we must explore a little since it is likely to prove one of the thorniest problems.

Traditionally, 'Brethren' have taken a very strong line on this matter. Though few among 'Open Brethren' would go anything like as far as Darby who wrote a celebrated tract entitled, 'The Notion of a Clergyman Dispensationally the Sin against the Holy Ghost', they have an almost instinctive feeling against it. Moreover, to them it would be little short of tragic if, at a time when churches with a long tradition of having it have become aware of its deficiencies, those which have long been wary of it should embrace it without reserve. It may appeal to some types of personality which find team leadership difficult and are natural, sole leaders. And it has some advantages (e.g., providing 'unity of command' as well as easy entry to the wider community). It is also arguable that it tends to happen in practice, anyway. (I seem to recall hearing the term 'leading elder' used on more than one occasion in the past.) But, without questioning for one moment the value of having one (or more) people working full-time in a church, it would surely be a retrograde step to move into a situation from which so many churches are trying to extricate themselves.

## POINTS TO PONDER

It may help to conclude by pinpointing a few fairly obvious things which may help those coming into 'Brethren' churches as full-time ministers.

1. Be at pains to provide clear evidence of your total commitments to God, scripture, the gospel, and the people to whom and with whom you are ministering.

2. To the best of your ability, establish good relationships with your fellow believers. Without partiality, try to make them your friends. Unless you and they work together in reasonable harmony, your

ministry is not likely to last very long!

3. Don't rush your fences. You may see half a dozen things that you would like to see changed. Don't try to change them all at once, and don't worry if hardly anything has changed during the first year or so. I have closely observed evangelical Anglican vicars who are appointed to non-evangelical churches, and they think in terms of decades rather than years as the time scale for significant change. The changes which they are seeking to bring about are, of course, considerably greater than those you may be contemplating, but there is an important principle here.

4. Don't imagine that *everything* needs to be changed! There may be things which need to be changed in *you*. Be on the lookout for aspects of the church which are admirable and should be conserved, as well as those which cry out for alteration.

5. Be reluctant to deal with issues head-on. Try to appreciate the feelings of those who value the past and the familiar. Hesitate long and hard before presenting them with hard choices, unless the ground has been well prepared. Instead of confronting them with arguments, whether biblical or not, and challenging them to an immediate response, prepare the ground in your biblical expositions and teaching sessions, planting seed thoughts, dropping broad hints, and working towards the end that *they* will suggest the things which *you* could have presented them with months before! And when it comes to reasoning with them, give them room to manouevre; don't force them into a position where they will 'lose face'.

6. You may find it easier to introduce new things in a totally new context rather than attempt to introduce changes into an existing one. It may be wise to maintain the old alongside the new, as long as there is a demand for the old as well as the new.

In all things, be wise as serpents as well as harmless as doves!

# Appendix 1

# Specimen Application Form

## *PASTOR*

### PERSONAL DETAILS

Name
Permanent address
Telephone number
Date of birth
Place of birth
Marital status
If married - how long married
        spouse's name
        date of birth
If children - names and ages

### PERSONAL GIFTING

1. How would you describe your personality?

2. What do you see as the gifts God has given you for this role in the church?

3. What attracts you about our vacancy, from what you know of it?

4. In what areas of a pastor's work do you feel you are less strong? (We ask this as we do not expect a pastor to be particularly gifted in all areas, and we would not want to have expectations which you may find difficult to fulfil.)

5. What is your personal vision for the next few years of your life?

6. How would you describe your spiritual life today?

7. What is your spouse's attitude to this application, and what role in the church would she like to have?

8. Please give brief details of any health problems, physical or psychological, which either you or your spouse have currently, or have had in the last few years.

## PERSONAL EXPERIENCE

1. Name and address of the church of which you are at present a member, and your role in that church.

2. Describe your experience in Christian work which is relevant to this vacancy, or attach a current CV.

## REFERENCES

Please give the name and address of two referees (preferably one personal and one church related). These references will be taken up at the appropriate time, unless you request otherwise.

# Appendix 2

## Reference Form

COVERING LETTER

*Please reply to*:

Dear
_____

has expressed interest in applying to work at this church as pastor.

The church has a membership of _____, with a Sunday attendance of around _____ adults. A very full programme takes place during the week, including various community projects, and a registered pre-school.

We are looking for a pastor who will lead the spiritual life and direction of the church, in partnership with a leadership team of _____ (including _____ elders and also a full-time youth-leader/pastoral assistant).

Responsibilities are to include preaching and public leading, overseeing the pastoral care of the church, and helping to lead the church forward in evangelism and discipling.

It is essential that the pastor is an experienced Christian, well able to work with a fairly large group of Christians from different backgrounds, in a harmonious and inspiring way.

We would be very grateful indeed if, in confidence, you could kindly speak for him by responding to the enclosed questions.

With many thanks indeed,
Yours sincerely in the Lord Jesus,
(Chairman of the leadership team)

## SPECIMEN REFERENCE FORM

Name of applicant

Name of referee

How long have you known the applicant?

In what capacity?

What can you say about the applicant's personal Christian experience and devotional life? To what extent would you consider that he governs his life by the Bible?

Does he show a helpful example in Christian home and family life?

Does the applicant show an example of consistent commitment to church life?

In what areas has he been committed consistently to Christian service?

Has this service borne fruit?

Have there been any difficulties associated with his involvement in the above?

Does he have a care and enthusiasm for evangelism?

Are you aware of any people whom he has personally introduced to faith in Christ and who have continued in discipleship?

Does he relate well with both Christian and non-Christian people?

Is he a man of vision (e.g., having foresight, suggesting fresh initiatives, bringing others 'on board', and seeing them through effectively)?

Does he cooperate well in a team-leadership situation (i.e., not tending to dominate, but working in fellowship with other leaders)?

Is he a good listener, and able to offer spiritual/biblical help to people in times of difficulty?

Is he well motivated, able to work on his own without supervision, maximising the use of his time?

Is he a leader (i.e.,does he make things happen, let things happen, or not know what is happening)?

How well does he handle conflict/disagreements?

Does he make friends easily?

Can he relate well with all ages?

What would you describe as the applicant's strengths?

What would you identify as the applicant's weaknesses?

Is he in good health?

Do you support his application for this position? (Please state if you know whether this is confirmed by the applicant's church leadership.)

Would you welcome him working full-time in your church?

Any other comments, please.

253